Breathe
Play Laugh

Health & Happiness with Humour

David Cronin

'Breathe Play Laugh' is exactly what we need to give us new ideas to add to our repertoires. There's already been some belly laughing today and I look forward to seeing how the team continues to integrate your ideas into practice.'

— Luana Passal acqua Acting Manager, CAMHS Western

'We are so happy with your work we are rolling it out to our other divisions here and interstate.' — Westpac Bank Executive

'I was awakened in the morning with the sight of five ladies on the golf course in their pyjamas. I heard them all doing a Ho Ho Ho and a HA HA HA. It was so funny!'

— J Moon, Community Health Service (HSFKI)

'The Convention was successful and reported as "the best ever" by many. David, The Clown Doctor, was an excellent speaker and demonstrator of "laughter is good medicine". You were the highlight of the conference.'

— Janine Keulen Kiwanas International

'I felt the condensed content delivered here gave my team a range of mechanisms and tools to be able to deal with work and life challenges.

'Your ability to get group participation and make a difference to the lives of the group was fantastic. They still talk about the Laughter Yoga, inventing all sorts of new HA HAHA, Ho Ho Ho. Thanks for making a difference.'

— Andrew Foster-Johnson TAFESA

Breathe Play Laugh

Health & Happiness with Humour

David Cronin

BPL

Copies of this book can be ordered via the author's website at www.davidcronin.love, booksellers or by contacting:

Breathe Play Laugh
davidcronin3@bigpond.com
www.davidcronin.love

ISBN: 978-0-6450656-2-6 (hc)
ISBN: 978-0-6450656-3-3 (sc)
ISBN: 978-0-6450656-4-0 (e)

A CiP number is available at the National Library of Australia.

Printed in Australia, UK and USA

rev. date: 31/03/2021

CONTENTS

DEDICATION

This book is dedicated to my parents, Pat and John, who taught me the value and virtues of family, and to my own family, with my heartfelt thanks for their support on my journey.

Mum had a zany sense of humour that could find fun in any situation. Dad's strong work ethic was dedicated to creativity and originality. This and his love of music, theatre and art continue to empower my life as a 'Heart-ist.'

Both had the courage to start a whole new life in another land on the other side of this planet, leaving all they knew behind. I'm forever grateful for their choosing Australia as my home.

One thing I have noticed: that taking sides while living on a circular globe makes as much sense as a chocolate teapot, or a screen door on a submarine, or...well, I trust you to discover your own sense of humour to answer this along our way here together.

'A sense of humour is the only divine quality of man.' — Arthur Schopenhauer

FOREWORD

I have been associated with David at a professional level for over a decade now. Every time that we met in person, I found another creative layer hiding beneath a very humble exterior. The only side of him that I hadn't seen of him was that of an author...and now I have.

This book is a reflection of David's playful and engaging personality. It captures the many levels of his talents in an easy to read manner, while providing activities that can be learnt and shared by people of any age and ability.

The clever layout of the book takes you on a journey back in time to when things were just... FUN! I read it from cover to cover with a smile on my face, interspersed with some laugh out loud moments. I hope his next book doesn't take as long to write as this one has ha ha ha.

Enjoy Life
Merv Neal
CEO Laughter Yoga Australia, Medical Author and Gelotologist

INTRODUCTION

Welcome!

Each of the seven chapters in this book has sections on Breathe, Play and Laughter. They connect and build on each other.

Each chapter aligns with one of our seven energy centres, or chakras. We start from the bottom up! Each has a colour of the rainbow, and these colour the breathing, the play and the laughter.

You will NOT be adding anything new to your life. You get moving by increasing the quality, not the quantity of these three elements, Breathe, Play, Laugh. How? Because we already do all three! You simply change the way you do them. You grow the fun at your own pace.

THE POWER OF THREE

The Tripod to Consistent Happiness

> 'Everyone should become rich and famous and have everything they've ever wanted, so that they can realize that it's not the answer.' — Jim Carey

What's that you're thinking? If you're like most people, reading this produces a reaction something like, 'Sure, but just let me try it first – the rich part I mean!' Do you see what you did? You have within you the power to spontaneously create this funny, laughable humour. This example may seem trivial, but it's a strength you possess, and you can use to your advantage.

Do you take your wellness as seriously as you take your work? We all like to perform well and be consistently good at what we do. That is what it means to be professional. So are you professional about your wellness? And how can you mix the serious with the playful? We face this paradox each day.

If you are grasping at happiness it will only elude you. Aim for consistency, not constant happiness. This means that you will have the ability to recover more quickly and smoothly from inevitable mood swings.

Happiness entails attention. It is estimated that 80% of the 12,000 to 50,000 thoughts you have every day are repetitious, and these vary from cautionary to negative.[1] You need powerful tools to gain traction in this quagmire.

Conscious breathing, playing, and laughing give you the leverage to create your mood.

Get your body moving and enjoy yourself! Any movement is good, but **having fun** is the most effective way to kickstart your day.

The Breathe, Play, Laugh Sequence brings you inner alignment.

It can be done in less than five minutes, three times a day. The best thing is, you make it a part of your existing routines, so you don't lose any time!

The Tripod System of Breathe, Play, Laugh integrates Body, Emotions and Mind into one whole. I call these your Home, Heart and Head.

The Breathe, Play, Laugh system is a script for you to put into action. Just as the screenplay for a movie is nothing but words on a page until it is brought to life by the actors and the whole

creative team, these words will have power only when you add your energy.

The strategies here are easy to use. You can start immediately and do them every day. The common thread that ties them all together is fun, and it's the reason you have the greatest chance of success with the system!

I suggest you do two weeks on each chapter, so yes, this is more like a manual. You can focus on our three parts – Home, Heart and Head – for as long as you like. Until you not only know and understand it, but internalise it as well, you make it your own.

THE FUN FACTOR

There is a feeling for many people that their world is spinning faster and faster, almost out of control. Depression is now the number one disease,[2] stress becomes chronic, and it seems like somebody else has their foot on the accelerator. Alongside stress, loneliness is becoming a real challenge for a growing number of people.

For many the task of maintaining their physical, emotional and mental wellbeing feels like constantly putting out fires. The core issues remain neglected. In fact, 80% of people who pay for a gym membership drop out within five months.[3]

So, how do you achieve health in your Home, Heart and Head?

This is where the Fun Factor comes in. Why? Because we tend to do more of what we already enjoy. If we liked doing something last time, our brain tells us to do it again. Science shows us that this basic mechanism of Trigger/Behaviour/Reward[4] is the same for all our habits.

Breathe, Play, Laugh is about being physically, emotionally and mentally healthy, because ultimately we all want to feel whole. And we also want to feel wholly connected to the people around us. With the correct dosage of Fun you will fly through the day!

Breathe, Play, Laugh is a simple system that you can fit into activities that you already do, like your morning walk, driving a car, or even while doing household chores! It takes just nine minutes a day. That's right, nine, which means you won't be taken out of your comfort zone with a jolt. It's more like shifting gears in a car. And I believe that Shift Happens!

You may have noticed I slipped an 'F' into the old saying. Do you know what the F stands for? 'Fun', yes, and also:

FLIP!

You can flip your mindset around as fast as flipping a pancake. This is the easiest, the most effective, and definitely the most economical way to get fit and stay healthy. And the fastest too! It's super efficient.

'FLIP' gives you the full tool kit: 'Fun Laughter In Play!' = acronym FLIP.

Breathe, Play, Laugh [BPL] integrates the body, heart and mind into one whole, allowing you to find your true alignment. The great interest now is in neuroplasticity. This ability of the mind to keep growing with exercise opens up new horizons. So BPL will:

- Free up more energy for the things you love.
- Bring joy to your whole being.

LIFE MAPS FOR THE JOY OF LIVING

Happiness is a whole science now, measured by more and more governments. Increasingly, Western countries have a department for asking people how happy they are. Australia comes up with an average score of seven out of ten,[5] which may be what you would expect – not outrageous, just sitting pretty.

But why not ten out of ten? After all, we're all in the top 1% of the wealthiest in the world. Perhaps there are far more factors at play when it comes to rating your happiness quotient than they put into the questionnaires.

With thirty years experience as a physical comedy performer and drama coach, I have developed a deep understanding that the *playful process* is the key. Drama is about telling stories, and these stories are about you and me. It is in these stories that each of us finds a connection, a relevance to our own life.

Our story helps us to map where we are and who we are, as well as where we are from and where we are going. You rediscover your vision and your values.

Once you learn this principle, it carries over into every aspect of your daily life. It is *your* story that you will discover here. Your story has the power to:

- Give you renewed hope and vision, to see clearly where you are going.
- Give you a firm foundation, to feel stable and grounded on your journey.
- Give you the resilience to keep going.

Above all, it reconnects you with your joy of living, and from there, you are able to connect more deeply with others.

1 FLIP

'To keep the body in good health is a duty, otherwise we shall not be able to keep our mind strong and clear.'

— Buddha

MOVEMENT AND CHANGE

It is human to have desires. You may want to be slimmer, richer, fitter or more successful; you may long to find true love; you may just wish to feel generally happier. Whatever it is, we all want some kind of change. There are numerous methods available, hundreds of them just one click away, and many of them are free.

So why don't we make the changes we need to get the things we want?

Essentially, change can be scary, because it means facing the unknown. Our greatest wish is peace and safety, and we can best remain in this state by keeping still. That is, by moving as little as possible.

We enjoy, and even need, some variety to our routine, but our over-riding desire is that things stay the same. We want life to feel secure and predictable.

This wish is a self-fulfilling prophecy, because the power of a belief means that we *literally* stop moving! We can't stop ourselves travelling forward in time, but we still keep our foot firmly planted on the brake pedal!

When what we want most is to remain in our comfort zone, the message we get is 'stay put!' We are continuously re-enforcing our subconscious belief that 'keeping still equals keeping safe'. We have a passivity bias, so there is no motivation to move.

If staying still feels comfortable and safe, what are the benefits of movement?

HOW TO CLIMB
THE MOVEMENT MOUNTAIN

There are numerous benefits to movement. These include:

CONNECTION

Connection can mean connecting with ourselves, as well as connecting with others, and the world around us.

Connecting with ourselves means integrating body, mind and spirit into one package. This is where we get our 'integrity' – it literally means being a whole person.

Becoming content with who you are, and how you are, is the best way to become connected. Although it may take a while to feel connected, the good news is that you are already whole, and you already have all the resources you need inside.

Notice that with 'inte-grit-y' you get the 'GRIT' built in. It's already there!

This does mean looking honestly at who you are, with all your faults and foibles, and learning to accept them. Only then can you start to 'tee hee' a little, and then to laugh out loud at them. Fuelling your *fun factor* and *play power* regularly to lift your laughter level will help with this process.

Connecting with others and the world means reaching out. It's good for you, and for those around you. Studies now show that the biggest factor for maintaining good health is connecting with others, and contributing to your community.[6]

Reaching out to connect involves opening up your heart and letting others in, so the bubble wrap must come off the package. Connections outside yourself can also be to places; which may be specific, such as a particular town or city or even a particular building; or general, such as being out in nature.

HEALTH

Humans are built to go. Your body needs movement to activate your lymphatic system. This is your 'waste disposal' mechanism, so it's important to keep it functioning well.

Your body produces a whole range of chemicals when you move. It's a complex mix, including endorphins, which are the feel good, pain-reducing chemicals. As well as producing chemicals, your muscles get a stretch, your organs get a shake up, and, in fact, every system gets activated.

FEEDING YOUR MIND – IMAGINATION & VISUALISATION

People are relying more and more on the plethora of entertainment to do the imagining for them. We are bombarded continuously with other people's stories. Most of us are happy to play the part of an 'extra' in everybody else's show but our own. We'd rather sit or stand around in the background and watch those who do move take the spotlight.

We forget that we are the star of our own movie. There are no rehearsals, and the camera is already rolling.

MOTIVATION BEFORE MOVEMENT

Many studies have shown that the number one priority for everybody, over a basic living threshold, is to be healthy.[7] This means either achieving or maintaining good health. We know instinctively that health equates to a better quality of life, not to mention a longer one!

So our motivation for movement is *quality of life*.

BEING AND DOING

When you want to make any kind of change that improves your quality of life, it is important to make a distinction between **being** and **doing**. Being and doing can both be active or passive. Movement does not mean that you need to be constantly **doing**. You can race around in circles and get nowhere.

Stillness is just as important when creating change. You need to be able to sit with yourself, even with your boredom, just **being**. When you are **being** you are aware of it, and give it your attention, rather than immediately wanting to distract yourself, just so that you don't have to experience the feeling.

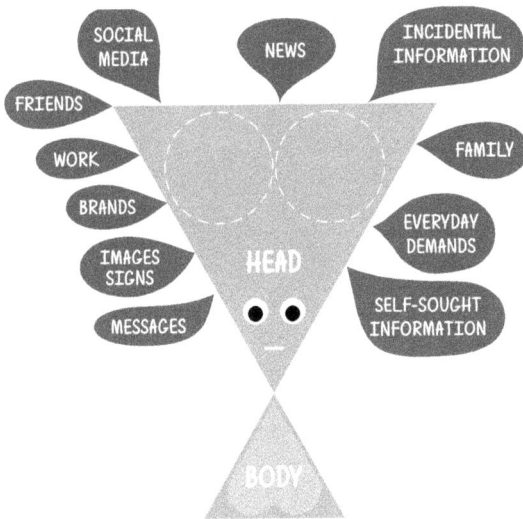

21ST CENTURY
HOMO-INFORMULATED

Taking the time to just **be** can help you move forward, just as constantly **doing**, without any thought or understanding of what you are working towards, can keep you from getting anywhere.

Take 'the pursuit of happiness.' If you repeat this mantra often you could come to believe that you must be moving. After all, being 'in pursuit' means that you're going after something. You may not catch it, but at least you're in motion, right?

KNOWLEDGE, DECISIONS AND ACTION

Knowledge is important, and may lead you to make a decision about what you want to do, but making a decision doesn't always result in taking action. When we are stuck in our heads there is a gap between the knowledge and the action. This gap allows the head to overrule the initial idea coming from your inner wisdom or instinct. We need strategies to 'beat our brain', so that we can quickly follow through on our intentions.

CREATING A NEW SELF-IMAGE

Step One – Creating A Solid Base

Okay, so you're motivated to move and improve your quality of life. To achieve purposeful movement, you need to change where your motivation is coming from, which means that you need to FLIP!

With information overload like a daily tsunami, our brain becomes so dominant that we often forget to check in with our physical self. If we could see ourselves as an image, we would look like an inverted pyramid, much bigger at the top and tapering down at the bottom.

The trouble is, this is not a stable form! The only way it can stay balanced is to keep moving, like a spinning top, which must keep turning because if it stops it will fall. We've all seen how such a top moves – its actions are erratic, with no clear direction.

Take the image of the top-heavy pyramid. Now flip it over, so that the base is at the bottom, and the point at the top, the way a pyramid should be. This is what you need to do to get out of your head and into your body, and have a solid, stable base to work from, so that you can move with purpose.

Many studies now show that your body, especially your gut area, has a far greater effect on your emotions than your brain.[8] This not only influences, but actually *determines*, our decision-making process, and the outcomes of that process.

Throughout this book, you will learn how to FLIP from your head to your body, using the principles of Breathe, Play, Laugh.

BREATHE

Breathing is the one certainty you have in life. It is constant movement, in and out. In fact, it may be all the movement a lot of us do! Looking at this in/out pattern, you become aware that *your breath is continuously flipping*!

It's changing direction constantly. Becoming conscious of this will help with visualising your 'top to bottom' flip.

Our breathing carries on regardless of our observation. But our breathing is one of the few bodily functions over which we have control. By taking the time to do some conscious breathing, you exercise control over your most primary action.

FEELING IN CONTROL

The major reason to breathe with intent is to take control of your life. To be in charge of the changes that must occur. This is perhaps our greatest wish of all: to steer our own direction.

SHIFTING FROM THE CONSCIOUS TO THE UNCONSCIOUS MIND

Meditation Made Simple – Method One

The first thing is to get into a quiet space where you won't be disturbed. Set aside twenty minutes if you can, but this length of time is not essential. You can start with as little as three minutes and gradually build up to twenty minutes.

Assume a relaxed position, so that you can focus on your breath. It is important to keep a straight back, to allow open access to your windpipe and lungs for your breathing. The ideal position is sitting up. However, you can do this meditation standing, sitting or lying down – whatever is most comfortable for you. If it helps to close your eyes, go ahead.

Now breathe in and out, counting each breath up to ten.

Thoughts will come. You can't 'stop' them. Simply acknowledge them without giving them any more attention, then return to the awareness of your breathing. This takes practice. So don't judge yourself, just keep practicing, and it will become easier.

One image from the East may be helpful. Imagine that you are a mountain, and thoughts come and go like passing clouds. You may observe them, yes, but they move on. Some may even thunder for attention, but they too dissipate, and you remain.

Work towards meditating every day at a certain time. If you miss a day it's no biggie, but remember that any habit needs repetition to get established, so aim for at least four of the seven days in a week.

Meditation Made Simple – Method Two

You will have already noticed that we need to breathe out the stale air, so that we can breathe in the fresh air. This means that we need to breathe out longer than we breathe in.

The best way to do this is to count. For example, breathe in for four, and breathe out for six, or eight if you can. It's up to you what ratio you do, as long as the 'in' breath is shorter than the 'out' breath.

You can try it now. As above, as with the first meditation, sit in a quiet spot, if possible. Now simply count the 'in' breath. Do what comes naturally here, don't force anything.

On the 'out' breath count a little longer than you did for the 'in' breath. You may find that a count of 5 'in' and a count of 7 'out' suits you at this stage. It may vary on different days, and at different times. Adopt whatever ratio is comfortable for you.

Hold On

When we hold our breath, our lungs get to absorb more of the oxygen than from a normal breath, which comes in and goes straight out. You can receive three to five times more oxygen from a held breath!

I recommend that you start with simply observing your breath first and getting used to this for a while, then doing the 'breath counting' meditation.

Once you are comfortable with counting your breathing, you can add holding your 'in' breath to your meditation, so that you increase the amount of oxygen you absorb.

Depending on what rhythm you choose, your count may go something like this: breathe in for four, hold your breath for five, breathe out for six.

Other meditation techniques include guided meditations, where you have an audio accompaniment to your meditation. This may be words, chanting and/or music. The sounds are typically gentle and repetitive, easy to listen to and devoid of distractions. There are also movement meditations, which can involve any kind of movement, from walking to dancing to yoga to running.

Daily Rites

Throughout the book you will find daily rites for breathing and laughter. These rituals are short, sharp and easy to remember. They are integrated into your daily routines, and are focused on finding the fun in the ordinary things you already do. As the saying goes, 'It ain't what you do, it's the way that you do it.'

Rainbow Breathing Rites

Red-Basic breathing: bringing your awareness to the breath, both the in and out breaths, as well as the moments of change between the breaths. Do not 'control' these, simply become aware of the process.

Aim for three minutes, or twenty breaths, to start with. You will soon extend this to twenty minutes when you add some Mind Empty (MindMT) techniques (as distinct from mind-full).

Play

Two important points to consider about play:

1. **Play involves the whole brain.** MRI scans show that it is not just some parts of the brain that are used when playing. The whole brain lights up! This is like having all the lights on in the house, and access to every room, while not having to worry about the power bill! This means that when we play we have total integration of all areas of the brain, and total availability of all its functions for problem-solving and creativity.

Whatever our form of play, it provides us with greater access to all parts of the brain, due to the increase in connections. Not only are all areas available, but the contacts between the two sides of the brain are multiplied.

This allows us to have a singular focus. We tend to play in what is called 'the zone.' This is a state of 'flow' that is exactly the same as the one reached by top athletes, and high performers in any field, be it business, politics or sport. It is an open, flexible state of mind, balancing readiness to change with sharp concentration.

2. **The purpose of play is to play!** The process IS the point. This means that *play should be open-ended. A result is not necessary.*

Play means being absorbed in whatever it is in that moment – the present. It's all about the journey, and not the destination. This may sound simple, but in practice it is the opposite.

Why? Our experience with sport gives us the best example.

We are accustomed to playing games that have a set structure and a result. They have a defined space, a set of rules, and usually a set time. And from a very early age now, children are brought into this competitive world of sport.

However, the world of play is different. It is at the other end of the spectrum. Adults who have been brought up on competitive sport find this very hard to understand, and even harder to allow it in their children, or those they have charge over. Yet we speak about 'playing' a sport.

This is the hardest concept for us to FLIP – play does not need a result!

We saw an example of this in the AFL Grand Final of 2010. When the siren sounded, and the game ended in a draw, over 100,000 people stood stunned. They were unable to fathom the possibility that the two teams were in fact equal and evenly matched. There was no mechanism left to cope with this real option. They insisted on a result.

It is well worth the effort to at least suspend judgement for a while, to regard this concept as a real possibility. There are enormous benefits to be derived from allowing the combination of fun and play to enhance learning in all areas of education.

Laugh

Researchers have found that people used to laugh on average nineteen minutes per day. That was over a period of fifty years in the twentieth century. By the end of the study it was down to just six minutes. That's a lot of laughter lost![8]

Where are we now in the twenty-first century, with people feeling 'time poor'? Down to five minutes of laughter or perhaps less? Do we have no time left to laugh? Is laughter becoming endangered?

Life's Laughs Lost!

After two generations of missing out on laughter, we tend to take this situation as normal. We accept the status quo. We consider it weird to laugh out loud, especially in public. We find it strange to laugh long and heartily. So how can we laugh longer and louder again?

To do this we need to FLIP our ideas about laughter over and over again, to discover what lies beneath, like turning over stones that have been lying in one place for too long.

By using the principles of Breathe, Play, Laugh to flip your motivation for movement from your head to your body, you will begin to send signals *from your body to your brain*. The action coming from below engages the pre-frontal cortex, which tells your brain that something new is happening, and drags the brain out of its default mode. This then enables you to start tailoring your movement to your life, which is where the Three R's come in: Relevance, Repetition and Revision.

Relevance

The activities you choose to do need to be relevant to your daily life. Choose the seven 'Breathe, Play, Laugh' steps that have the most meaning for you, and then simply link these steps with things you already do!

Repetition

Momentum is the power that comes from starting and keeping going. It creates its own force, and it feeds on itself, so that it grows bigger and stronger the more you do it. And when you enjoy the playful moves you'll want to repeat them!

Revision

Revision means looking at and celebrating what you have done. Whatever it is, no matter how small, celebrate your achievement. Every seed is important, and has the potential to grow, so give it thanks and praise, dance and cheer, give yourself a hug, and repeat a favourite affirmation, such as, 'I am amazing!'

> By linking your Breathe, Play, Laugh activities to your routine activities they will gradually grow to become part of your Daily Rites.
>
> Breathe, Play, Laugh activities don't need to be done all together.
> It's better when they are spread throughout your day.
> That way they act to reinforce your momentum.
>
> If you don't do every activity every day, that's fine.
> Doing a little is better than doing nothing at all!

BREATHE, PLAY, LAUGH ACTIVITIES

Wake Up and Laugh

If you want to get up and get moving, use this simple device. Here's how it works: when you laugh, you bring your brain straight to the here and now. You snap it into a state of unconsciousness, because you're literally connecting your gut and your head.

This brief rite is done with short, sharp sounds. See if you can do it with one breath. It need not be loud, but it does need to be expressed.

Take a deep breath and go:

'HO, HO' – 'HA, HA' – 'HEE, HEE' – 'HA, HA' – 'HO, HO.'

It rises up and returns down, from one base point to the high point, and back to the other base point. These form a triangle, which flows over the pyramid in the diagram, helping to keep you flipped the right way. It moves away from, and returns to, the base.

Seven Chakras Laughter – Root Chakra

These laughs align with the seven chakras, or our 'energy nodes'.

For the HOME we laugh, 'Hoo-hoo-hoo.'

The 'Hoo-hoo-hoo' is the laugh of the root chakra, at the junction of your legs. The 'hoo' is pronounced like an owl's 'who'.

Tips

You do not need to worry about getting the laugh 'exactly' on the chakra point at this stage. That will come as you are more comfortable and familiar with your body.

Variation

I recommend that you have a go at doing each laugh three times, rather than twice. That is, 'Hoo-hoo-hoo' rather than 'Hoo-hoo'. This helps with the flow, by taking your mind away from the regular two-beat rhythm. Perhaps also there is something about the '¾ beat', which we associate with dancing.

If this doesn't feel comfortable then you are welcome to stick with two, or perhaps try four laughs. It's all about finding your own rhythm, and feeling the fun in the laughter.

To start with you'll probably want to focus on laughing with your chakra, and this is easiest to do when sitting or standing, however you feel most comfortable. Later, you may find you also enjoy doing these Chakra laughs in a variety of ways, for example when you're out walking, or doing daily chores.

Rainbow Laughter Rites – Red

1. **Make A Fire:** Laugh as you mime making fire without matches, by creating sparks with flint stones, or rubbing a stick between your hands like a drill.

2. **Hot Coals Laughter**: Walk on red-hot coals, breathing sharp, short breaths as you keep moving and getting to the other side.

3. **Red Light Laugh:** Laugh like your car engine with a steady rhythm as you drive along the road with a regular 'internal' laugh. A 'red light' ahead and you have to stop! A 'green light' and you take off again. Meet two more red lights and laugh, then you're there. So get going!

'Teach us delight in simple things.'

— Rudyard Kipling (1865–1936)

2 SHIFT HAPPENS!

It can feel uncomfortable when things start to shift. One thing that can help is to know that the word 'happens' is related to the word 'happiness'.

So 'Shift Happens' is simply another way of saying that change is our only certainty in life, so why not enjoy the ride, rather than gripping on tight with both hands and white knuckles?

We change the meaning of the old saying by adding the 'F' – this time for 'Fun'. The purpose of adding the fun can be applied to any situation that requires change. There are three simple steps that you can follow:

- find the fun
- embed it into any situation
- deal with it effectively and empathetically.

Once you're ready to embrace change, you're ready for the next stage in creating a more accurate picture of the relationship of your head to your body.

So far, we've created a solid, stable base, which represents your body. However, you still need to engage your mind. Once you're confident that you are connected with your body, you can bring your mind back into play. Keep everything in proportion, though. To do this, imagine that you are placing a smaller upside-down triangle on top of the larger right-way-up bottom triangle. This smaller, upside-down triangle represents your the head.

Now you have a far more accurate representation of the relationship between your body and your mind, with the lower part, your body, as the dominant player.

Of course, there is a continuous loop of communication between the head and body. In order for this communication to be effective, you need to keep this channel clear. So how do you achieve this? One key component is meditation.

'Sit quietly doing nothing, spring comes, and the grass grows by itself.'

You may have thought that by SHIFTING we would be going up through the gears, like the good old manual car. But this SHIFT is from the conscious to the unconscious.

Our conscious mind is only the tip of the iceberg when compared with the vastness of our unconscious mind, and the shift we are making is into the largely unexplored territory of unknown dimensions. This is where meditation comes in.

It is easy to think we need to stuff every moment of our lives as full as possible, as if it would be negligent to do otherwise. After all, we never get any of that time back again. Time runs on and disappears if we don't use it, right? This is the mentality in Western culture, especially since the industrial revolution, when 'time is money' became the overriding belief.

It is only in fleeting moments that we catch a glimpse of nature and are reminded of the passage of seasons or the life cycle of animals. It may be the death of a pet or the fluttering wings of an insect that captures your awareness. Suddenly, you remember how fleeting life can be.

When asked what he had gained from meditation, the Buddha replied, 'Nothing.' 'Nothing?' the people asked. 'That's right,' he repeated, 'nothing. However,' Buddha continued, 'let me tell you what I lost. Anger, Anxiety, Depression, Insecurity, and Fear of old age and death.'

There is now overwhelming scientific evidence that practicing meditation has enormous benefits. But if you are like most people, you baulk at having to sit still for twenty minutes.

We are so used to having at least one electronic device going, if not three at once. How can you cut yourself off from your phone for two minutes, let alone twenty?

Well, I can only emphasise the awesome power you will gain through meditating regularly.

There are many methods available, but we will focus on some simple techniques with breathing as the basis.

BREATHE
Fun First!

Let's remember that fun comes first. We'll employ the wonderful power of our imagination to make these more than 'exercises', by turning them into continually new and enjoyable experiences.

This awesome power is generated in our subconscious, which is far bigger than our brain, and even bigger than our mind. It is in every cell of our body, and even reaches beyond that, flowing back and forth with waves of energy.

By tapping into this source, we can connect our subconscious with a wealth of resources to our conscious mind!

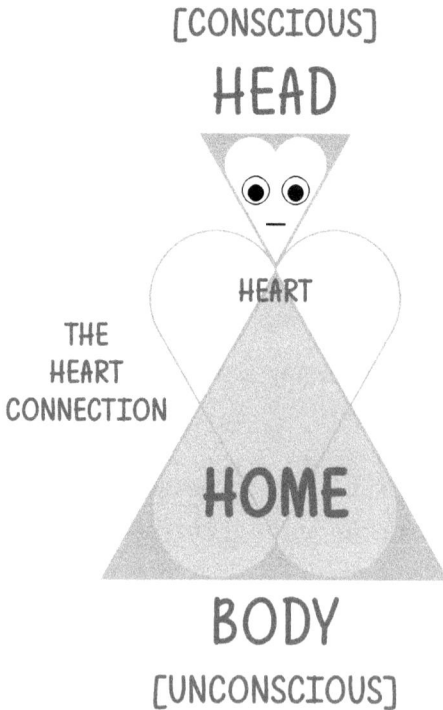

[CONSCIOUS]

HEAD

HEART

THE
HEART
CONNECTION

HOME

BODY
[UNCONSCIOUS]

SHAKER DANCE

This is especially fun in a group, and with your favourite music playing. Start by shaking your hands gently. Now find a rhythm to this.

Add your forearms, then your whole arms, then shake your shoulders.

Keep adding body bits until everything is shaking.

Now add the laughter for a silly dance. Move around and meet others, or just fill the space if you're on your own.

Here are some more images to get moving.

THE PUPPET

This time you're a puppet on strings controlled from above.

Do you feel as though you always need to be in charge?

Or are you willing to be manipulated into doing a silly dance?

In this exercise, you get to be the puppet and the puppeteer as well!

This exercise involves being aware of your head, your chest, and your lower body. Just let the rest, your arms and legs, dangle and be pulled and jerked by the strings.

It is okay to take responsibility for your foolishness. That way you can balance the serious with irreverence.

In the end the decision is yours. It is you who chooses to be free. You are not the freedom, or the silliness itself. You are the whole person, the total being. And you do have a choice between the silly and the serious. In fact, that's exactly where the choice is, *in between*.

You have the flexibility to move in either direction. You can choose how silly you get, or how serious you want to be.

You can imagine a 'spectrum', or scale if you like, ranging from one extreme to the other.

Do not be afraid to take enough control to dance with delight, making your own steps. They may be faltering, baby steps to begin with, as you start your new path.

THE RAG DOLL

This is a fun way to let yourself go all floppy. Imagine you are sitting there, waiting to be picked up and hugged. You may be asked to carry out some tasks, with a little help, or you may simply be there to comfort someone.

THE DRUNK

The character of the drunk dulls the senses. Drugging the senses probably acts as a diversion from any real, underlying problem. It may be that the person was hurt, wounded in the head, heart or physically. So rather than risk being hurt again, the drunk denies the pain and covers it up.

Beware! Sometimes those who are carrying broken heads or hearts may lash out in anger. They may even take on positions of authority, so that they can better hurt others! And this in itself becomes an addiction – the aphrodisiac of power!

Do not confuse these drugs of delusion with the choice of freedom. This can be such a liberating force that it appears to others that you are drunk on life!

Move as though you are going through the different stages of drunkenness, from alcohol or drugs, to power, to freedom.

The Tree

Stand with your feet planted, and sway like a tree. Take both the gentle breeze and the blasts of the wildest storm.

You can feel rooted and secure in your contact with the ground. This is your basic beginning position, to know that, essentially, you are one with nature.

No matter what spirit you see within yourself, your body is the vessel or vehicle for all you do. Your energy can and does extend beyond your body. But like it or not, this is where you live. It is up to you whether you see this as a temporary abode, a house you are merely renting, or a home.

Trees are also the source of many of the things that you receive. The tree bears fruit, gives shade, and even provides you with the air you breathe.

By reconnecting with your natural self, you are validating your basic nature, which is not separate, but encompasses all energy. We know now that science has finally rediscovered this, what we have known all along. That in each cell of our body there is the same energy, the same patterns in every atom. These very same patterns are replicated, right up to the stars in our galaxy, and across the universe.

Rainbow Breathing Rites – Orange

Dawn Breathing: take a deep inhalation and make a big smile as you open imaginary curtains to a new day. Let the sunshine in. Rejoice at what you see. Laugh out loud. Then open another imaginary window and repeat. Do this a few times.

Aim for three minutes, or about twenty breaths, to start with. You will soon extend this to twenty minutes when you add some MindMT techniques.

PLAY

Shifting Our Perception of Play

> 'To play is to take something – anything – on its own terms, to treat it as if its existence were reasonable.' – Ian Bogost

We think that in play we 'do what we want' – that we free ourselves from external duty and obligation, and yield to our innermost desires.

But freedom is not an escape from limitation. Games aren't appealing because they are fun, but because they are limited. It is the very limitations of games which makes them fun. Having boundaries gives you a framework within which to explore.

Play isn't the opposite of work. It is our approach to things that allows us to play. Anywhere can be a playground, and when we understand this, we give ourselves the opportunity to cultivate humility and acceptance, because play requires us to treat things as they are, rather than as we wish them to be.

At its very core, play is not selfish, but deep and deliberate. When we play, we engage fully and intensely with life and its contents. Play bores through boredom to reach the deep truth of ordinary things. Play means approaching life with attention.

Play Can Be The Secret To Contentment

Children play constantly. Two of the most important reasons for this are that they seek joy, and they are constantly adjusting to an environment that is not theirs.

Play isn't doing what we *want*, but doing what we *can* with the materials we find along the way. Play helps us develop a greater respect for the things, people, and situations around us, which allows us a far greater level of contentment in our lives.

So, what is the key to play?

Play begins when you take an object, event, situation, or scenario that wasn't designed for you, that isn't invested in you, that isn't concerned in the slightest about your experience of it, and then treat it as if it were.

Play Deprivation – The Seriousity Epidemic!

We are currently experiencing what I call a 'seriousity epidemic', and when you consider the following facts, it's easy to see why.

- Children up to the age of four are naturally intuitive, infinitely creative souls. By the age of eight or nine they enter another stage.

Developmental psychologists such as Jean Piaget have argued that children do not develop the general cognitive capacities for probabilistic inference and hypothesis testing until concrete operational (age 7–11 years). It is possible that this can 'take over' and diminish our intuitive capacities.

Why do we play less? Well, play is seen as belonging to childhood. We move on, grow up, and leave it behind. But play is an essential element at all stages of life. It is one of the key ways in which we learn. Not only that, but science now shows that without a daily dose we can suffer from play deprivation; in the same way we would from sleep deprivation.[8]

The Rise of The Robots

To enable robots to walk like us, their creators closely study human movement. They find that what we do is actually 'fall' forward when we walk, and then catch ourselves. We swing one leg through, and shift our weight onto it while we swing the other leg through.

So we are virtually falling and rising again, over and over. Humans have in effect a 'third leg' when we move, formed from the action of the other two!

That third element is that briefest of moments between when the shift happens, from one leg to the other. Just as there is a flip, or shift between one breath and the next. Of course our forward motion compensates for this, and we smooth it out as much as possible.

Many robot designs feature a third leg, which swings through while the other two support it. This is the basic feature that enables robots to move over any terrain, no matter how difficult.

Robots are also destined to afford us much more free time in the very near future. But it's not just about the fact that we will have more leisure time available to us. We need to get proactive about how we will bring fun, play and laughter into every moment of our lives right now.

Laugh

Do you have a 'WAIT' Problem?

How many people wait for something or someone to change their life and bring them happiness? I think more people have a 'wait' problem than a weight problem! But you don't have to wait to be happy. Laughter is your birthright.

Laughter Super Powers

Laughter unlocks 'Super Powers' that you already possess! They simply need releasing and nurturing. By tapping into your laughter, you will feel your powers growing. Regular laughter allows you to access:

- **Super Speed**: Laughter provides perspective to see new possibilities and solutions.
- **Super Connection**: Laughter shatters barriers, opens up social communication and connects you to others.
- **Super Vision**: Laughter helps you harness creativity for solving problems and innovation.
- **Super Strength**: Laughter enables you to develop the resilience to face life's challenges.

You may feel that there's not much to laugh about in this world. There's taxes, terrorists, tragedies, troubles – and that's just the 'T's! If you've been caught up in the seriosity epidemic, that's okay, you can still be cured, because one of the wonderful things about laughter is that you can 'fake it 'til you make it!'

Laughter involves the part of your brain responsible for pleasure. The really good feeling you get from laughter is provided by a set of chemicals, in particular dopamine, endorphins and serotonin. Interestingly, although smiling doesn't have the same aerobic benefits as laughing, it still produces the same 'happy' chemicals.

When your body has a pleasurable experience, it wants you to repeat the action, so that it can get another 'high'. When it comes to laughter, your body wants it so much that you can initiate the same reaction simply by acting out the physical motion of laughing or smiling.

Try it now. Smile. Feel it. How easy is that!

So does laughter really lead to happiness? One thing is for certain, laughter leads to health. It's been shown in many scientific studies with a wide range of groups that there is a definite and lasting improvement in all aspects of health, from pain relief to longevity. And good health is one of the basic pillars for happiness. As Albert Schweizer said, *Happiness is nothing more than good health and a bad memory.'*

Add these 'Low' Laughs to your tool kit.

Santa Laughter: Hold your belly and give the deepest 'goodwill to all' laugh you can as Santa.

Big Friendly Giant Laughter: Be the tallest giant you like and give a friendly, rumbling laugh that reverberates far and wide.

The Seven Chakras Laugh – Sacral Chakra

For the HOME we laugh, 'Hoo-hoo-hoo, Ho-ho-ho.'

The 'Ho-ho-ho' is the laugh of the sacral chakra, just below your navel. The 'ho' is pronounced 'hoe,' like Santa's 'ho'.

Rainbow Laughter Rites – Orange

1. Pick oranges from a tree with laughter. Pop them in your bag or basket.

   Peel and smell the oranges with laughter.

   Juice them by twisting your wrists – swap hands to use both sides.

2. Imagine you are watching a sunset, breathing deep and sighing at the beauty. You can make a ring for the sun with one hand's fingers, and a horizon with the other arm. Let the sun slowly sink, and laugh as you imagine vivid orange colours lighting up the sky.

   Better still, go out at that time and watch the real thing, laughing at the glory of this change from day to night.

3. Hop like a bunny rabbit around the carrot patch. Dig up a juicy carrot and enjoy munching it with laughter. But keep a watch out for the farmer!

'Nothing can cure the soul but the senses, just as nothing can cure the senses but the soul.'

— Oscar Wilde (1854–1900)

3 CONNECT

THE HEART CONNECTION

Now that you have formed a clear connection between your body and your head, you can bring the third component – your heart.

You will see that the double triangle, which is formed by your head and your body, has now become an infinite loop that is reshaped by your heart. By creating an infinite loop, you can follow the same path until you have developed an established pattern that becomes second nature.

Why is this important? When forming a habit, most people do something new once or twice, and then give up. The first time is a novelty, and therefore it is exciting. The second time you recall that feeling of excitement, and want to recapture it. After that, you are wired to seek something else. Your brain says, 'Got it, let's move on to the next thing.' This concept is my own, based largely on the fact that most songs people hear are a similar pattern. They have two verses with the same melody, and then there is a 'need' to change to a new tune, which is often the chorus. The need to persevere regularly, even without novelty, for at least ten weeks on average is fairly widely accepted now.[9]

So taking that third step is tougher than expected.

When you engage in an activity for the third time you are creating a habit. Each time we repeat a thought or action it reinforces that neural pathway. So just like a bush track becomes a major road through constant traffic use, your habits establish themselves in the same way. And just as a better road makes for easier driving, once you have a clearly established habit, it becomes easier to keep up with that way of thinking or behaving.

So repeat your favourite breathing, playing and laughing activities again!

BREATHE

Fuel For Freedom – Maximise Your Oxygen

You can go for days without water, weeks without food, but only minutes without air. Breathing is the very essence of our life.

Air = Life

As simple as this equation seems, it's true. Breathing is a necessity just like eating. The vital ingredient that you are taking in from the air is oxygen. But why do something consciously that is going along just fine as a subconscious action? With conscious breathing you will breathe better. You breathe deeper and longer. Why is this good?

The main reason to breathe consciously is to increase your oxygen intake. You may think you get enough, but in reality, if your breathing is shallow then it becomes restricted to chest muscles only. This means that you involve only the top third of your lungs at the most, and take in just 20–25% of your total lung capacity. The residual volume of air, the remaining 75% that stays in your lungs, is old and stale. Oxygen is the fuel of life, so it is essential to flush out this stale air and fill your lungs with the riches on offer. [10]

Reduced oxygen intake leads to the accumulation of carbon dioxide, which can in turn further increase stress. This is not just a vicious circle, but a downward spiral for your health.[11]

Your brain alone needs 20% to 25% of your oxygen intake. That's a huge amount, although your brain is less than 5% of your body weight. It's a hungry beast![12]

The biggest contributor to this hunger is your relatively new relationship to screens. You may not be aware that when looking at TV or computer screens, your phone or a screen of any kind, your lung intake goes as low as 2%! You've virtually stopped breathing![13]

The majority of us spend at least five hours a day in front of a screen during our leisure time. Add the time you spend in front of a screen for work or study, and it really adds up![14]

One huge reason to take a long, hard look at how you breathe is that the positive impact on your health can be enormous.

Two specialists in the field of aerobic medicine, both of whom have been awarded Nobel prizes for their work, have this to say:

> 'Deep breathing techniques increase oxygen to the cells and are the most important factors in living a disease-free and energetic life. When cells get enough oxygen, cancer will not and cannot occur.'
> — Dr Otto Warburg

'Oxygen plays a pivotal role in the proper functioning of the immune system. We can look at oxygen deficiency as the single greatest cause of all diseases.'

— Stephen Levine

This is great news for your health and wellbeing!

The Secret To Deeper Breathing

The secret to breathing more deeply is more about exhalation than inhalation. When you exhale longer than you inhale you ensure that you remove the carbon dioxide from your body.

This means getting your diaphragm and abdominal muscles going. They help activate the parasympathetic system, which is the calming branch of the autonomic nervous system.

The parasympathetic system is, logically, the opposite of the sympathetic system, which is the stress arousal system. The beautiful thing is, your body only does one at a time. So moving your diaphragm switches off the stress arousal system and switches on the calming system.[15]

It takes only thirty seconds to establish a new neural connection in our brains. This initial link is the first, but when you repeat the same action continuously the pathway gets reinforced, and what was a footpath turns into a road, and then a super-highway![16]

Rainbow Breathing Rites – Yellow

Breathing: breathe out longer than you breathe in. (e.g. When you breathe in for four 'counts,' breathe out for six.)

Aim for three minutes, or about twenty breaths, to start with. You will soon extend this to twenty minutes when you add some MindMT techniques.

PLAY

'Isn't Play Just Play?'

To CONNECT completely with play we need to trust it, and that means getting to know it better. The first question to ask is this:

What is the Opposite of Play?

Like most people, you will probably answer that the opposite of play is work. But this relatively recent concept came only around the end of the 19th century, with the concept of dividing the day into equal thirds, eight hours of work, eight hours of leisure, and eight hours of rest. This is a by-product of, and a reaction to, the industrialisation of the workforce.

However, even if you have a nine-to-five job, you still have to commute, maybe be on-call, clean work clothes, do chores, and so on – and that's all in our leisure or 'play' time! The separation between work and play isn't so simple.

Underneath all this lies a fact that we may not be aware of: we are programmed to play. We are hard-wired to learn, and we learn by having fun. It's not only the best way to learn, it's the only way. This applies throughout our lives, not just when we are children. It is how our brains work. Play is our FUNdamental birthright.

Play Is In Our DNA

Our brain can suffer from play deprivation in much the same way as it can suffer from sleep deprivation. The brain only truly switches on when we play.

That is, when we do something that is different, that has an element of discovery or, in other words, something that is fun. Without this vital element the brain literally shuts down, and goes into 'sleep' mode.

No wonder we find routine boring. So, as much as we need structures and schedules, plans and deadlines, our brain also craves excitement. The sad thing is, often we see this as 'naughty' and may feel guilty about it, especially if we make choices that can adversely impact on our lives in order to get the stimulation we crave.

The truth is, we all play games, all the time. The sooner we accept this, the sooner we can move beyond the shame, blame and name games, and make a conscious, informed decision about having real fun.

So the opposite of play is not idleness, boredom or work. It is the inability to engage with what we have; a passive disconnection that can spiral into depression.

Definitions Of Play

Play is as much in the approach as in the activity. It implies a sense of fun, but can also be serious, in two senses:

- The person may feel serious while playing, and/or
- The content of the play may be serious, that is, not trivial or light-hearted. Much free play is reflective.

The twentieth-century development of psychoanalytic thought emphasised the role of play in coming to terms with, and mastering, disturbing experiences. Through play, 'fear becomes a source of enjoyment rather than distress'.

It is believed that children under ten years of age have at least twice the synaptic capacity as children over ten. This plasticity has been linked to the effects of enriched environments. This increasing understanding of the working of the brain is also leading to a reassessment of what is now called emotional intelligence, and is giving rise to suggestions that play in young children may have a critical role in the enlargement of brain capacity.

Benefits that are experienced at the time of playing:

- Provides opportunities to enjoy freedom, and exercise choice and control over ones actions.

- Offers opportunities for testing boundaries and exploring risk
- Offers a very wide range of physical, social and intellectual experiences

Benefits of playing that develop over time:

- Fosters independence and self-esteem
- Develops respect for others and offers opportunities for social interaction
- Supports wellbeing, healthy growth and development
- Increases knowledge and understanding
- Promotes creativity and capacity to learn.

LAUGH

Laughter and Food – How To Lose Weight By Laughing!

We have a natural desire to eat as much as possible whenever food is available. This mechanism arose in times when food was only available intermittently, and we still have the same body physiology, and the same desires. Nowadays food is available to us whenever we wish, although we still have the same need. So the question is, how do we discard these desires that we no longer need?[17]

Taking a long look at the food you eat is so much easier when you laugh. Why? Because laughter changes your perspective on everything. Regular laughter enables you to not only look on the bright side, but to look at things from many different angles.

This means that, almost without thinking about it, you will start to review what and how much you eat!

It is easy to obsess about *what* and *how much* you eat, but stressing about what you eat and how much you eat is far more damaging for your health than actually consuming the food itself![18]

Two other factors that are just as important as *what* you eat and the *quantity* you eat are *how* you eat and *when* you eat.

How You Eat

Laughter will let you enjoy your life more, which means that you make the experience of eating special. How you eat your food becomes a delightful process. This allows you to listen to your body. As you eat more slowly, savouring the tastes and smells, your body is more able to tell you when it is satisfied. By eating more slowly you also get other benefits. You enjoy the sumptuous tastes more, and you give your digestive process the best start it can get by chewing your food properly. This reduces all sorts of strain on your digestive system, which takes less energy away from your total food intake.

When You Eat

With more laughter in your life, you find that this regular release of emotion deals with many of the underlying causes of overeating and comfort eating. Laughter lets you feel these emotions, so that you are able to deal with them and heal them.

Laughter allows you to access the root of the problem, and not simply cover, dampen and deny it. You become so busy with fun activities and relationships that meals become a seamless inclusion!

Habits such as snacking to compensate for negative feelings that you are holding inside, binge eating or missing meals to punish yourself simply drop away.

Laughter As Exercise

When we laugh, we use our diaphragm and our abdomen. This is the major muscle mass in our middle, front and centre. It is also the site of our major fat storage!

Laughter uses this muscle mass solely and completely.

Normally with exercise we use this muscle to move others: to stretch, pull, bend, lift legs, and to walk. With laughter, we focus exclusively on this muscle mass, and we move it to the maximum with the principal purpose of expelling the stale air from our lungs.

The intensity of laughter is greatly underestimated. The aerobic benefits from ten minutes of laughter are equivalent to thirty minutes on a piece of exercise apparatus, such as a rowing machine.

This means laughter is three times more effective than exercise apparatus! And best of all, laughter is free and it's FUN!

How Much Laughter Do You Need?

You do need enough laughter to start the physiological changes. They need to be real belly laughs – sustained and continuous. That is, not just a snicker, giggle or a snort for a few seconds, which is all we normally do in response to a joke or a funny situation.

You need to consciously do the rhythmical motion of laughter for at least ten to fifteen minutes a day.

This is where Laughter Yoga comes in. By taking the action of laughter as a fun breathing activity, you can do it for as long as you wish.

You may choose to laugh for ten to fifteen minutes in one go, or you may choose to do several shorter lots of laughter, spread out over the course of the day. For example, you could do four minutes of laughter three times a day. It is up to you.

Seven Chakras Laughter – Solar-Plexus Chakra

For the HEART we laugh, 'Ha-ha-ha.'

The 'Ha-ha-ha' is the laugh of the solar-plexus chakra, at the base of your ribcage.

RAINBOW LAUGHTER RITES – YELLOW

1. **Banana Laughter**: Smile as you peel a banana and look forward to enjoying every bite. Suddenly a monkey grabs your banana and runs away! Laugh as you get up and chase him!
2. **Sunshine Laughter**: Fling the curtains open and laugh as the sun streams in. Go around and do this to each room in the house.

Next we're going to get right to the heart of the matter.

> 'There is a child in each of us wanting to laugh at life. Let that child out to play as much as you can!' – Anon

4 YOUR DIAMOND CORE

'The body is your temple. Keep it pure and clean for the soul to reside in.'
— B. K. S. Iyengar, Indian yoga founder

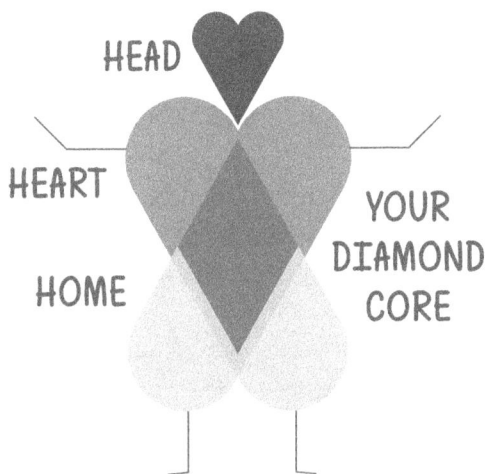

HEAD

HEART

HOME

YOUR
DIAMOND
CORE

Once you have created clear patterns and pathways that allow you to establish new, healthy habits, you can begin to go deeper, and allow your heart to take its rightful place – at your centre. The diamond that forms here is your indestructible core. As you can see from the diagram, the pathways have many options, so you can have fun dancing around your diamond.

'The part of us that we imagine needs healing is not the part we create from; that part is far deeper and stronger.
The part we create from can't be touched by anything our parents did, or society did or does. That part is unsullied, uncorrupted.

It is soundproof, waterproof, and bulletproof.
The part that needs healing is our personal life.'
— from 'The War of Art' by Steven Pressfield

Besides their resilience, diamonds are valued for their brilliance. So as you breathe in, take in light as well as air. As you breathe out, laugh as you shine brighter with every breath!

Science has now shown that your heart is more than a pump. In fact, your heart can create emotions and tell the brain what to do about them.[19]

The brain has been subjected to extensive study, and much is being learnt. The brain is of course part of the body and is extensively connected to the body through various feedback mechanisms.

The heart has also been the subject of steady research, and amazing discoveries have been made. For instance, the heart has its own intrinsic nerve/neuron cells to regulate cardiac activity.

The heart is constantly transmitting feelings to the brain, e.g. when our heart races it makes us feel anxious, just as anxiety can make our heart race.

Your heart is also a major endocrine glandular organ, producing its own hormones, and also produces its own electricity – on average, two-and-a-half watts a minute.[20]

This creates an electromagnetic field. The energy produced includes power waves, similar to radio and light waves, which comprise the principal source of information upon which the body and brain build your neural conception and perception of the world.

It is within this field that you will attract those who you want around, your 'tribe'. They're the ones who share your energy, who nurture it and inspire you to be your best. The combination of all your energy fields creates a 'synergy', which is itself energising.

This is when 'the whole becomes greater than the sum of its parts'. Just like the compound interest generated by an accumulated sum of money, there is an extra, indefinable bonus from being part of a team.

BREATHE

Lose Weight By Breathing! [21]

Your body possesses its own intelligence, and has incredible healing power.

Somatic Intelligence

The emotional intelligence of the heart is vital for your relation-ships and community connections. And the head's analytical intelligence is useful, and well worth training.

However, by trusting in your somatic ('of the body') intelligence, which you may call your 'gut feelings' or intuition, you tap into a vast source. This is important for so many areas of life, such as relating to others, parenting and making decisions.

Somatic intelligence is engaged when you connect with your core values, and when you discover and act on your true passion.

To make the discovery requires getting in touch with your body, and one of the best ways to do this is through playful breathing.

Simple Breath

Breathe in, drawing the air deep into your diaphragm. This is your centre, or your core. Feel your breath filling the space like an empty vessel. Do this three times, breathing in and out, until you can feel your breath going directly to your core.

Make sure you are not holding your breath, keep the flow going. Release any tension in your neck and shoulders, and check the rest of your body for tension. For example, you may be clenching your leg muscles more than you need to.

This exercise can be done as often as you like during the day. I recommend that you do it at least three times.

Set aside particular times of the day, such as before meals. You could also do it every hour, on the hour. You can do this exercise sitting down, although ideally it is best to stand up and get your whole body involved.

As we focus on where we direct our breathing the exercise becomes a mini-meditation. The very act helps us concentrate our mind.

Breathe in, taking the air deep into your core. Feel it filling the space. Do this three times, breathing in and out. Now count up to five breaths. When you're ready, go for seven. You may feel your back moving as well as your abdomen. Allow this natural movement to happen. Enjoy the rocking action.

If you want to imagine that you're rocking on the ocean go right ahead. You won't get seasick from this!

Moving your breath to your core may feel unfamiliar, but over time you will recognise the sensation, and the exercise will become easier.

Two Hands Breath

This breathing exercise is simple but very powerful. You check here that your breath comes and goes mainly from your core.

Place one hand on your heart, and your other hand on your solar plexus. As you breathe in, aim to have only your bottom hand lift, breathing as deeply as possible. Check that your upper hand on your chest hardly moves at all. Repeat seven times.

Humming

Humming gives us the same benefits as laughing, singing, dancing and playing. This is a fun variation, because you can play at being a buzzy busy bee, flitting among the flowers!

The vibrations give us a wonderful massage, and they give our body and spirit a great message too. You can enjoy just feeling these vibrations by placing your hands on various parts of your body as you hum.

Take a deep breath, and as you hum put your hand on your head, then your chest, then other parts of your body. Check how it feels in different places.

You can also try out various humming pitches, moving from high to low.

Take My Breath Away

Singing is one of the best fun ways to breathe better, since we bring our whole self to the process: body, heart and soul. I recommend taking every opportunity to sing out!

Rainbow Breathing Rites – Green

Awareness Breathing: encounter a moment of beauty every day. Stop, take three breaths to settle, and then count ten breaths while focusing on the beauty before you. You will not only become more aware of the detail, you become more aware of your body.

There are a whole variety of ways to use this simple technique. Here are a few more suggestions: You can sit and bring to mind your own happy image, and focus on this while doing the ten breaths, and you can also focus the energy to any part of your body which needs it.

Aim for three minutes, or about twenty breaths, to start with. You will soon extend this to twenty minutes when you add some MindMT techniques.

PLAY

Play Personalities, Properties, And Process – The Control/Chaos Continuum

Your story is yours alone. And the kind of player you are at your core is a unique combination of your upbringing and your experiences. Far from being merely a leisure activity, as we now perceive it, play is the primary reason we are here.

Without the retelling of stories, our species could not have advanced to the level we have reached. This power of repeating stories, the original method of passing on knowledge from one generation to the other, is what defines us as human.

You are defined by the stories you tell about yourself. Your daily actions are the story that you show to the world. To better understand yourself, it helps to look at the person who is telling these stories. That's why you can look at Play Personalities, and the process of play.

You probably know that the best way to make a story interesting is to make it entertaining. As in this story about Truth.

'A storyteller called Truth had a collection of wonderful stories, and wanted everyone to hear what he had to tell them.

Even though he was totally naked, he went to the marketplace in the nearest village and began to speak. Nobody stopped to listen, so he headed to a nearby town, found a prominent spot in the square and spoke as loudly as he could. Still no one took any notice. He then travelled to the capital city and shouted his stories to the crowds that thronged the streets. But the people there also quickly disappeared. Then he heard a voice.

'Hey, you' the voice whispered. Truth looked around and could see no one. 'Psst, over here,' the voice called.

He saw someone beckoning to him from the shadows, and cautiously went over. 'Who are you?' Truth asked.' 'I'm Story' the stranger replied. 'If you want people to listen, put these on.'

Story handed him some colourful clothes, and Truth put them on. When he looked around to thank her, Story had disappeared. Truth stepped out of the shadows and began to speak again. He spoke clearly and strongly, and this time people stopped to listen. The crowd grew, and everyone enjoyed his stories. They gave him food and money to travel further. After that, Truth carried the clothes with him and put them on whenever he reached another town.'

The message in this tale is that the best way to learn is through play. This has been understood for a long time, as we can see from the Ancient Greek word for education 'paidera/paida', which means 'play'. In each of us there is a wide spectrum of 'players'. These are Play Personalities, and by understanding your play personality, you can not only gain a better awareness of yourself, but also extend your range! By getting out of a fixed pattern of 'play' that may be boring for you, and for those around you.

PLAY PERSONALITIES[22]

The Collector

The collector is focussed on assembling and/or maintaining a collection of interesting objects or experiences. This may be done alone, which would be the case with someone who had lots of figurines, or with others who have similar interests, by swapping trading cards, for example.

The Artist/Creator

Making things is the focus and source of joy for the artist/creator. Arts and crafts of any kind fall into this category, as well as inventing, designing, decorating, and constructing. Creations can be functional, artistic, or simply playful.

The Storyteller

This personality focuses on imagination. For those who love to read, write, draw, or watch movies. The storyteller is able to create an imaginative world that can permeate almost any activity or context, from telling jokes through to making up children's games.

The Director

Planning, organising, orchestrating scenes and events are the favourite activities of The Director. This Play Personality prefers being the puppet master. Activities include making a meal, fundraising, creating home movies, and planning parties.

The Joker

Represents the most obvious and often the most extreme of the Play Personalities. The Joker adopts an inherently fun, silly, nonsensical style of play, which can often be outrageous. They may come 'alive' only at certain times.

The Kinesthete

The focus for this Play Personality is on movement. These players include athletes of all description, as well as those who are most alive when on the move, taking part in activities such as dancing, hiking, swimming, and running. For The Kinesthete, it's not so much about winning or losing as being engaged in physical activity.

The Explorer

Exploring can be physical (going to new places) or intellectual (discovering new ideas or information) relational (meeting new people) or emotional (searching for a new response to art, or to a story).

The Competitor

This Play Personality engages in competitive games with the object of winning. The competitor likes to keep score, and typically likes to come out on top. It's important that the primary objective remains on play, fun and engaging together.

Play Properties

There are a number of different properties to play:

- Voluntary
- Inherent attraction
- Freedom from time
- Diminished consciousness of self
- Apparently purposeless (for own sake)
- Improvisational potential
- Continuation desire

Play Process

The play process has distinct stages:

Before:

- Anticipation
- Surprise

During:

- Pleasure
- Understanding

After:

- Strength
- Poise

The Control/Chaos Continuum

Throughout our lives, we all oscillate between control and chaos. In order to survive we gravitate towards the 'control' end of the spectrum. We strive not to 'descend' into disorder.

There are a number of positive outcomes from this way of being, but there are also negative repercussions. Essentially, always seeking to maintain control does two things. Firstly, it locks us into position, disabling flexibility.

Secondly, by constantly moving towards 'Control', there is always a compensatory effect, a re-balancing mechanism. When this energy finds no outlet, it will create subconscious sabotage in the order and discipline you struggle to keep.

This 'Control/Chaos Duality' creates a pattern of polarisation that resonates in every aspect of our lives. However, opposite ends of a spectrum need not be opposing antagonists. Only through play can we gain the flexibility needed to move, as desired, along this spectrum.

We should not see the 'Control' aspect of our brain as negative. It is there to keep us safe, to check on our actions and keep us alive. It's how we've learned to cross the street, and to judge situations and people.

The trouble is, it's in control of most of our brain, and is our default position. It can easily take over, unless we take regular action to redress the imbalance.

LAUGH

A Matter of Laugh and Death

When you get enough laughter in your system you tend to see things in perspective. You can be inspired by even the tiniest speck of joy in your day.

Sure, some days are rougher than others, but rather than seeing yourself as either 'the dog or the tree' recognise that there is a third option. You can be the observer, the one telling the joke about the dog and the tree. It is this that forms perspective on any situation, no matter how big or how trivial. It is through this that you achieve balance.

You have the power to choose how you perceive what happens. Often in life, it is not so much the challenges confronting us, but our reaction to them, which creates stress and pain. Even if we are aware of this, it is 'human nature' to make excuses, and to blame other factors, rather than taking full responsibility.

When juggling all the complexities of modern life, some upsets and cracks in the overall plan are inevitable. You spend much of your energy just on the logistics of getting through each day. As a result, it is easy to become obsessed just with organising the continuous flow of information, and easier still to become stressed and anxious when things go wrong. However, it is precisely these 'mini' troubles and frustrations that should get us laughing. The way to do this is to recognise what is actually going on. Only then can we learn to put the focus into a healthy place.

Your real challenge is to accept that you are not fixed. You are fluid energy. You are a constant conundrum! You are vibrations, so why not be 'good vibrations?' To enjoy every moment as play is your true state of being. Balancing your life, and juggling all your facets becomes the new game.

It is easy to get discouraged in life, and to settle for what we have, in the belief that it is safer in the middle ground. The point is not to have a safe position, but quite the opposite. In truth, **flexibility is the key.** If you have the ability to move in either direction when required, you are better able to keep your balance.

The energy inside you will align with the energy forces around you. The more you open up to these forces, the more you will find peace within yourself.

Bruce's Story

Bruce was 88 when he joined our Laughter Yoga Club. He told us of the time he was a farmer, doing it tough out in the marginal Mallee lands, with little to show for his backbreaking work. One day, at the end of a particularly hard week, he was returning a machine that he had borrowed from a neighbour. When he arrived they were just sitting down to lunch, and they invited him to stay, so he accepted the kind invitation. The food, wine and conversation flowed, and Bruce laughed so much that afternoon that he was still sore from it the next day! But he also felt that something had gone. The knot in his guts, that tight bundle of anxiety and anger at the battles he had waged daily just to survive, that knot was gone. He had learned the incredible power of laughter, and he never forgot it!

Calming the body affects both the heart and mind, as we know from meditation, but laughter has many more benefits, one of which may be lowering blood pressure.

Blood Pressure Heads South!

Part of my work took me into hospitals as a Laughter Therapist, or Clown Doctor, where I witnessed an incredible phenomenon a number of times. When I shared laughter with a child whose vital signs were being monitored by a machine, their blood pressure would drop. The look of surprise on the nurse's face was always entertaining! Contrary to medical expectation, laughter, rather than 'over-exciting' the child, would relax them.

Seven Chakras Laughter – Heart Chakra

For the HEART we laugh, 'Ha-ha-ha, Hey-hey-hey.'

The 'Hey-hey-hey' is the laugh of the heart chakra, in the centre of your chest. The 'hey' is pronounced 'hay'.

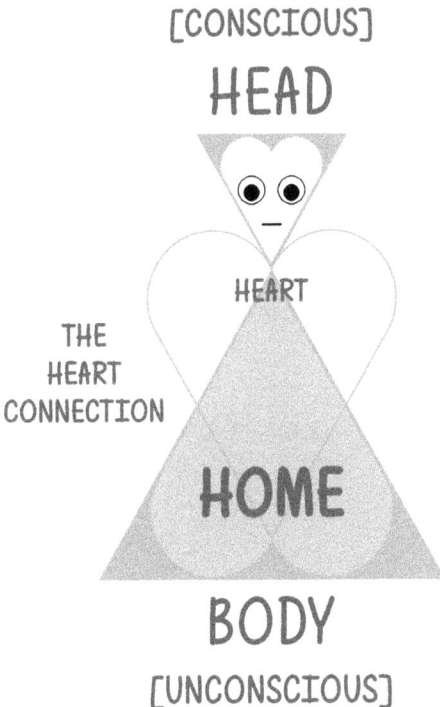

[CONSCIOUS]
HEAD

HEART

THE
HEART
CONNECTION

HOME

BODY
[UNCONSCIOUS]

Rainbow Laughter Rites – Green

1. **Heart Expansion Laughter:** Cover your heart with both hands and laugh from soft to loud as you slowly open your arms wider and wider.

2. **Hearty Laughter:** Make an elongated "aeeee" sound as you slowly lift both arms all the way up, then laugh heartily with your hands pointed to the sky. Imagine that your laughter is coming straight from your heart.

3. **Healing/Body Scan Laughter:** Be aware of any aches, discomforts or itches that you have – don't push them away, just be aware. Laugh from from that area of pain or itch and imagine that some of the discomfort is exhaled with the laughter, leaving your body.

'I know not all that may be coming, but be it what it will, I'll go to it laughing.'
– Herman Melville

5 ROLL UP!

'Our bodies are apt to be our auto-biographies.'

— Frank Gelett Burgess (1866–1951)

So far our model has created simple connections between our head, body and heart. Now it's time to take a step into the third dimension!

You can start with a fun way to get out of bed in the mornings. You may be familiar with the cries of the spruikers at the circus announcing the start of the show with 'Roll up, roll up!' Well, that is what you are going to do!

Both the Moshe Feldenkrais and the Alexander Technique will tell you this is the safest, easiest, and most economical way to raise your body from lying down to standing up.

It works like this. Firstly, you get down into your diamond heart with three deep breaths, in and out. It is this core that we move first, gently rolling sideways. Most people are used to leading their movements from the head and shoulders. By now you should be able to take your focus deeper into your body and hold it there. Next, rock and roll your core towards the side of the bed. Rock back once to the other side. On the third roll you're out and up and off.

BREATHE

Don't Relax, Release!

This is one to do with a partner. Lie down on your back in a fully comfortable position.

Breathe in and out, letting go of any tensions you may feel in your body.

The following exercise is to target any other tensions that are unconscious, and to release them as well.

Have your partner gently lift and lower each arm, holding on carefully with both hands. Your partner does this in a safe, caring manner.

Avoid any rhythms. Move the arm in deliberately unpredictable ways.

Vary the length of the moves, making some short, some longer.

Repeat this for the other arm, and then do both legs.

Throughout the exercise, make sure you breathe! When lying down this is the one thing that you focus on, nothing else.

Of course your partner gets to swap over and to enjoy this breathing muscle relaxation experience too!

When you feel comfortable with each other, you can also add this neck relaxation.

Sit above your partner lying on the floor and cup their head very carefully in your hands. This must be done very slowly and only with very slight movements.

Raise their head just a little and lower it gently. You can also do tiny sideways rotations. Ensure that these movements are always kept both slow and slight.

Rainbow Breathing Rites – Blue

Wave Breathing: like the waves lap into the shore and roll out again, our breaths have their own natural rhythm.

Aim for three minutes, or about twenty breaths, to start with. You will soon extend this to twenty minutes when you add some MindMT techniques.

PLAY

Giving Yourself Permission To Play

When people come to a laughter club, the first thing I say to them is 'Hello and welcome! Please give yourself 'permission to play.'

We're looking for anything that will let out more laughter. Otherwise it builds up, and the pressure can have nasty side effects, such as humouroids!

This is 'pure' laughter, without any reason. It's not about anyone or anything.

The Four Pillars Of Joy

Along with laughter, singing and dancing, play is one of the four pillars or principles of joy. All four are the foundations, and they support the wonderful experience of Laughter Yoga.

The biggest barriers to playing as an adult are the inhibitions we've built up while growing up. If a parent's normal 'negative bias' – as psychology calls it today – comes into play, it is possible that children could get up to five times more negative messages to one positive while growing up.

These are not necessarily abusive messages or 'put-downs', but simply parents warning their children to 'look out', 'don't touch', 'stay away from that', and so on. Many of these things are considered the 'normal' stuff of parenting.

However, this 80/20 ratio for the sake of safety has a real bearing on how we play.

'NO PLAYING ALLOWED!' – MYTHS & MESSAGES

There's an old folk tune that goes, 'Mama don't allow no banjo pickin' around here!' The verses continue in the same vein, substituting any activity you can think of as the one that mama don't allow. The song has a fun twist, with the end of each verse going: 'I don't care what mama don't allow, going to play my banjo anyhow.'

Take a look at the following messages. You can even say them out loud. Try reading them in different voices, as a serious 'parent' character, and then in a silly, fun voice.

Take a moment to consider which ones resonate with you. If any of the phrases are familiar to you, when and where did you hear them, and from whom?

- "There is an appropriate time and place for play and laughter"
- "Grow up and stop being so silly"
- "I can't afford the time to be frivolous"
- "You'll embarrass yourself"
- "Church is not the place for frivolity or laughter"
- "You shouldn't laugh at someone else's expense"
- "You can't laugh or play by yourself"
- "My laugh sounds weird"

It's easy to see why we need to plan to play more. Unless we are aware of all this programming we've been subjected to for so long, we will go on in the manner to which we are accustomed.

LAUGH

The Science of Stress and Laughter

Do you have enough laughter in your life?

Just as we may forget to love, if we forget to laugh often enough we soon experience life as a hard struggle. It is the spirit of laughter that animates acts of daily kindness, and boosts self-esteem.

Is laughter like soap bubbles, here and gone? Is it effervescent, ephemeral, lasting only a few moments long? Well, the science is in. Laughter doesn't go away, it hangs around.[23] Yes, laughter is not only feel-good medicine, it also has long-lasting effects. As the Norwegian's say 'Who laughs, lasts!'

Laughter's for the birds!

B – Builds body systems, including your immune system

I – Increases your perception, perspective and productivity

R – Reduces stress, improves resilience and resolve

D – Dissolves barriers and self-limiting beliefs

S – Stimulates communication, connections and creativity

Just as the birds start every day with a song, we can begin every day with laughter, no matter how we feel! As we cram more and more into our days, what often gets pushed aside first is the fun and laughter. Yet it is now proven that these are precisely what we need to handle the growing stresses of modern life.[24]

Laughter burns off tension to expose the pain

We now know that stress turns into tension that is held in our body. Yet we still wonder where these physical aches and pains come from. The great news is that the physical movement of laughter releases this muscle tension. Dr Jane Yip, a researcher at Australia's Newcastle University found similar results to those of Dr Fry, who showed that one hundred hearty laughs are equivalent to ten minutes jogging![25] Dr Fry, from Stanford University, is considered the father of Gelotology – the study of laughter.

A good belly laugh is an internal massage. It tones up every bodily system – the lungs, the blood circulation, and the nervous system are stimulated, and a whole raft of chemicals is produced in the brain. These are the positive, pleasurable, pain-reducing chemicals such as serotonin, dopamine and endorphins.

The amazing thing is that **these effects last.** Doctors Berk & Tan showed that these bodily changes remain not for minutes or hours, but all day! Even twenty-four hours later the increase is still measurably high, and similar to the increase you initially achieved. So the effects of laughter are sustained right throughout your day.[26] So all you need to do is to 'top up' the next day!

What is even more amazing, they found that **your immune system is strengthened.** That is, your body's ability to fight infection gets stronger!

Laughter stimulates the production of immunoglobulins[27] – no, these are not something out of *Lord of the Rings*. They're your very own defence from bugs and viruses. They come with significant numbers of reinforcements, to increase your chances of living longer!

Laughter is the most effective, efficient and economical way to wellbeing and staying healthy.

Chronic stress destroys your immune system

Stress is not simply an overload of thoughts. By taking on too many things at once, we produce a cocktail of real chemicals in our body. In too many cases today, this is becoming **chronic stress.**

The word 'chronic' means 'continuing over time'. That is, stress accumulates in your body, just like toxic heavy metals such as mercury and arsenic, which collect and remain, building up until they impact on every aspect of your health.

Chronic stress wears the body down. Common symptoms include: a weakened immune system; high blood pressure; stomach ulcers; skin problems; digestive difficulties; and impaired memory.

Chief among the chemicals produced is cortisol, which is responsible for keeping your sugar levels up! This is to give you extra energy for all the things you do.

Which is fine, until your body keeps craving more and more sugar.

We need to literally start the production of our feel good chemicals in order to release them. Here's the most amazing fact of all. Even if you're not very good at controlling your thoughts, or meditating and such like, you can actually control the chemicals inside your body!

Here's how...

Your brain is not one but really three parts. And the main brain is not involved in this process. What is involved is the primitive part, called the hypothalamus. This is your pleasure centre. This ancient section of our brain works very simply. It can only produce one response at a time!

That is, either it is producing stress chemicals OR happy ones, it can't do both at the same time. It's a one-way track. Just like the switches that take a train onto a siding, your stress response is side-tracked and de-railed when you input positive, happy, peaceful, calming thoughts.

What about 'multitasking', you ask? Well, all of that happens in the other parts of your brain, at the other two levels, especially your brain's highly developed frontal lobes.

It's important to emphasise that at this basic level the body/brain doesn't recognise the difference between simulated, created laughter and the real deal. So you can 'fake it 'til you make it'!

With this knowledge, we hold the controls on our own happiness. If you are wondering how you can laugh when you're hurting inside, the answer is that this is precisely when we need laughter most – in the hard times! The fact that we can only have one or the other, stress or happy chemicals, explains why it is so difficult for us to come out of a slump, but once you realise that you have your hand on the controls, you can switch the lever over to laughter whenever you choose.

It all began for modern times with Norman Cousins. He was diagnosed with an extremely painful back disease, but rather than lying in hospital being pumped full of drugs, he checked himself out of hospital and into a motel, where he watched funny videos. After only a few weeks he found that from half an hour of laughter he got two hours of full pain relief.

Other studies have now replicated this. For example, an arthritis group meeting monthly to laugh finds that their members need less medication.[28]

And in a study of forty-eight heart-attack patients, ten patients in the control group suffered repeat heart attacks after one year, compared with only two in the group that watched comedy shows for just thirty minutes a day.[29]

These benefits are produced from a full, hearty belly laugh. But when we laugh at a joke it is usually only for a few seconds, if that. So how do we get consistent, prolonged laughter regularly into our life?

Laughter Yoga provides an easily accessible tool to do just this. You can even laugh alone, with Laughter Meditation.

Laughter Yoga is purely and simply about:

- The health benefits, keeping fit in a fun way.
- The pure joy experienced by making a habit of laughing.
- World peace, because this begins with finding your own inner peace, and then sharing it.

Laughing Out Loud In Public – The Peinlich Paradox

Some people find it strange to be asked to laugh out loud for no reason. Even with all these explanations about the health benefits, we have an inherent need to remain in our comfort zone. We have a built-in wariness about the unknown. It is a normal and natural way of keeping ourselves safe, but it can too easily keep us in the control mode, and we miss out not only on the fun but also on the health benefits.

There is a trick. Rather than seeing this ability of ours to check everything as negative, simply view it as neutral, but useful for its purpose. Once you have experienced letting go and laughing for yourself, you will never be the same. From that time on, whenever you do laugh, you will allow yourself to laugh longer and louder than before.

You can use a bit of extra laughter whenever you have some fun in your life. Whether it is with people, jokes, some frivolity, or even on your own. Just the knowledge that you gain from reading this book will you enable you to laugh more frequently and more fully than you have done in the past.

The truth is, deep, long laughter is not really something new, it is just complementing what you already do. It is also regaining your 'normal' or natural level of laughter.[30]

Get The 'Ha-Ha Habit'!

The beauty of Laughter Yoga lies in regular sessions of laughter, making sure that you get your daily dose. By repeating the ten to fifteen minutes of laughter for fifty to seventy days, you will have the habit!

This is the experience of many trainers from all sorts of fields. Some people will learn more quickly than others, but basically, we need to do whatever it is we wish to learn for an average of at least forty days, in order to establish it as an on-going habit.

Seven Chakras Laughter – Throat Chakra

For the HEAD we laugh, 'Hee-hee-hee, hi-hi-hi.'

The 'Hee-hee-hee' is the laugh of the throat chakra, which is found on your neck. The 'hi' is pronounced 'high.'

Rainbow Laughter Rites – Blue

1. **Ocean Laughter:** While laughing, sway from side to side, rocking like a boat on the ocean.

2. **Tropical Waterfall Laughter**: Close your eyes. Laugh as you imagine taking a shower under a warm tropical waterfall.

3. **Avoid Fishing Hooks and Laugh:** While laughing, swim around imaginary fishing hooks in the water. This is a great metaphor for learning to avoid life's obstacles.

4. **Washing Machine Laugh:**
    Switch on the washing machine – press your belly button and laugh!
    Wash cycle: laugh with a low 'Hoo, Hoo, Ho, Ho!'
    Rinse cycle: laugh from your heart with a 'Ha, Ha, Ha!'
    Spin cycle: laugh really high with a 'Hee, Hee, Hee!'

'What matters is that one be for a time inwardly attentive.'
     — Anne Morrow Lindbergh, American aviator and author (1906–2001)

6 ROLL OUT!

'Come forth into the light of things, let Nature be your teacher.'
— William Wordsworth

Your journey through this book began by flipping your mindset into finding more fun and laughter in play, in order to enrich your life.

The sheer delight of movement itself is a joy, but the reality is it helps to have a reason. We all love a fun challenge or a dare, and there's no bigger challenge than overturning long-held beliefs that are due for a flipping change.

You only have to look at movies set in the forties and fifties to see how common smoking was. Yet today people view smokers with anything from pity to contempt!

Another example is the rise of the plastic shopping bag. Taking your basket to market was normal in the beginning, until plastic bags were provided free. We got out of that habit of taking our own baskets or bags for so long that it's taken decades to get *back into* the habit. You still see many people entering a supermarket without them, expecting to be served and sorted by the shop owner.

The point is, flipping our mindset with rather trivial items like this is an ideal way to keep us mentally flexible. It gives us an edge when dealing with the bigger challenges we face emotionally and physically.

Take our perception of a bright sunny day. How does it make you feel?

For the vast majority of people sunshine lightens their day. We smile and enjoy the life-giving warmth. On the other hand, an overcast, wet day has the opposite effect. A common reaction is complaints about the cold, and a dampened mood that can range from resignation to downright disgust.

Yet every drop of rain should be thankfully received as a bountiful blessing! We should celebrate every shower, we should be out there, dancing and singing in the rain.

This brings us on to 'Rolling Out' – which is all about communicating and using your voice. When it comes to the physical aspects of communication, other than taking air in and letting your voice out, your head has precious little to do with the process.

Your voice comes from your lungs and belly to begin with, and out through your throat last of all. Of course, your diction and head resonance do come into play, but unless you intentionally want a 'head voice' or falsetto, or a nasal country twang, your head does not have much of a role to play in this.

It is now time to roll out your Three-Heart Plan. This is where the three hearts are revealed on the walls of the pyramid. As you can see, the hearts fit into the three triangular walls of the tetrahedron upside down.

Starting at the widest part of the heart, you can track your progress.

Check off how you are doing in each of the three areas: breathing, playing and laughing, as you go through the seven chapters, and record your results in the three hearts.

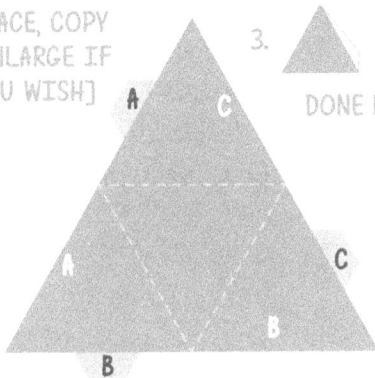

1. CUT OUT &
FOLD ALONG
DOTTED LINES

2. TAPE OR GLUE
TABS A B & C TO
POINTS A, B, C.

[TRACE, COPY
& ENLARGE IF
YOU WISH]

3.

DONE !

A   C

A   C

B

B

YOUR TETRAHEDRON TEMPLATE

TO COLOUR IN!

Beginning at the widest part of the heart, move upwards to the tip. Make a note of each time you do your breathing rites, as shown in the example.

You track back and forth, moving towards the tip from side to side. Notice that the distance decreases each time. This represents how we need to put in more effort to begin with, and how it gets easier the more often we do something!

You can think of it as the base camp for a climb. Without the proper preparation, a mountaineering team cannot succeed. You need to set up your base camp so that you have all the provisions and equipment to go on and achieve your objective, which is to reach the summit. You know that without adequate supplies you cannot reach the peak. Each stage of a climb is calculated carefully, planned with precision, and you need the correct amount of resources to recover each time and proceed further.

At the peak lies your head, and it's a long way to the top. So all the preparation begins at the base. It is important to get the first move right. Because it is from this first move that the rest follow.

BREATHE

80/20 Fits Us All

It's important to remember that most people only use around 20% of their lung capacity in a normal day, When you are looking at a screen this goes down to just 2%! Yes, you virtually stop breathing!

This 80/20 ratio is so important. Not only in relation to the amount of oxygen you take into your body, but also how you use it. Your brain uses 20% of your oxygen intake, yet only accounts for 3-5% of your body weight. It's a hungry beast!

The ratio also applies to your thoughts, with around 80% being repetitive, compared with 20% fresh, new thoughts. Notice that these are not judged as 'negative' and 'positive' thoughts. At the most they can be seen as 80% cautious and 20% creative.

A similar ratio can be applied to the 'Control/Chaos Continuum', which is a way of seeing your thoughts projected outwards, rather than looking inward.

Because the vast majority of our weight loss is through breathing,[30] you can apply this ratio to your daily fun exercise regime as well.

In simple terms we need three areas of exercise-stretching, strengthening, and aerobic. Applying the 80/20 ratio, you would be exercising:

10% Stretching

10% Strengthening

80% Aerobic

For ten minutes of exercise this means that you only need to be doing one minute each of stretching and strengthening, and eight minutes of laughter!

For the aerobic exercise you now have the knowledge to appreciate that laughter is the best way to do this. It's the most effective and the simplest method. It's also something you can do anywhere, at anytime, so it's the most immediate.

For stretching, look at the basic three moves:

Standing upright, gently twist the body with a sideways turn. Keep the arms loose and take your impulse for this move from your core.

Secondly, tip your body from the waist to each side.

Thirdly, roll down forwards and come up again. You can also gently bend backwards.

At all times start slowly, and always remain conscious of your breathing along with the movements.

For strengthening it is good to remember that you have your own body weight to use. You don't have to wait until you have any special equipment. Whether you do lunges, squats, push-ups or leg lifts, it is your body that gives you the counter balancing resistance to do these moves.

The 80/20 ratio is not a rule, it is just a handy guide. It was discovered by an Italian economist in 1896 and named after him as the Pareto principle, or Pareto distribution. While it has found widespread use in many areas including business, there are three things to note:

1. It is not a 'law' but simply a useful tool.
2. Both parts are not necessarily the same things, in fact they are usually different things.
3. The numbers appear to add up to 100, but that is not a constant. So the % sign is misleading. It is a ratio, and this 'joint ratio' can be 80/30 or 80/10 in some cases.

The main point about this ratio is that this uneven distribution is much more typical than we realise. We tend to think of things as averaging out over time. We believe that things should be equal and fair.

This averaging out is best described in a 'bell curve' diagram. Yet in reality many things in life are in this uneven ratio, what is called a 'Power Law Relationship'.

You only have to think of wealth distribution, which is what sparked Pareto's interest initially. He found that 80% of the land in Italy was owned by 20% of the people. His interest piqued, he discovered that this applied around the globe as well.

Of course it's the old adage – the rich get richer. However, we now know that this statistic is shrinking even more. The point for you here is not global, but personal, perception.

This book is designed to enable you to remain open and resilient, and to keep the ratios under control, by staying aware of the ways in which your physical, emotional and mental wellbeing are affected.

Keep using the exercises and strategies regularly to create a ratio that is as evenly balanced as possible.

RAINBOW BREATHING RITES – INDIGO

Nose Breathing: holding one nostril closed at a time, with either forefinger or thumb.

Aim for three minutes, or about twenty breaths, to start with. You will soon extend this to twenty minutes when you add some MindMT techniques.

PLAY

Fun At Work

This may seem like an oxymoron, but increasingly, corporations are wising up to the need to keep their staff happy. Simply on a business level, it makes sense. It costs five times more to hire someone new than it does to put strategies in place and care for the wellbeing of those you already employ.

There are basic things that should seem obvious, like having 'chill out' zones. These can be 'pop-up' or permanent places

– gyms, play-spaces, sport courts – even a mini table tennis table. A portable play trolley can be filled with fun objects.

A noticeboard can share fun cartoons and stories. And the opportunity to spend time with colleagues at the printer or in the lunchroom is important too. This means the manager allowing time outside of designated breaks, which is a matter of discretion. But it goes both ways. Staff will respect the chance to have fun at work. It all begins at the top, with trust and fun from the leaders. This will strengthen the relationships.

Too often, the focus is on reducing the amount of sick leave taken by employees, which is gradually creeping upwards as expectations keep increasing. But perhaps by putting our focus on sickness we are only giving it more energy!

I know one business owner who allows his staff to take three 'happy days' off work every year. If they are feeling too happy to come in, they simply have to call and tell the boss.

Not every boss is going to give their staff 'happy days', and even for those that are lucky enough to have that option, three days a year still leaves a lot of time when the focus is on work!

PICK A CARD

One way to ensure you keep an element of fun in every day is to program in times to play. Treat each hour like a pack of cards. After fifty-two minutes tell yourself that it's time to play. Remember those extra cards, the jokers that came with new decks, and you didn't know what to do with them? Have them 'pop up' at your work, at your desk or on your phone to remind you!

Eight minutes may seem like a long time to 'waste' out of each hour.

But when it is put to constructive use in a planned play activity, this time spent away from work will return major dividends, by delivering fuller focus for the following fifty-two minutes, re-energise you to contribute more, and helping you to avoid a range of distractions that would take up more than eight minutes if you added them together.

The best results come from activities that you can do while standing. There are simple moves that can be done on the spot, such as juggling.

Three reasons why having fun at meetings is essential

1. It is scientifically proven that people learn far better and are more attentive in a fun environment.
2. Energy is up, so connecting is easier.
3. Communication and creativity flow, for maximum contributions.

The same reasons apply whether you have to stand up and present, or whether you are selling something.

Often, people in this situation concentrate on only one thing: content. They want to demonstrate their knowledge and command of the subject. They need to show they are the expert, and dazzle you with facts from every angle.

There are two more essential aspects to getting material across, besides the content. These are **context** and **concept**.

HOW TO FIND FUN IN ANYTHING, ANYTIME, ANYWHERE

Repetition

If you repeat something often enough it does two things. Firstly, it gains an absurd or abstract quality – try it by repeating any word or short phrase over and over. You may have already done this and know the feeling! Secondly, it gains a rhythm of its own, a pattern which is appealing, due to its uniqueness.

Exaggeration

This is the mainstay of many a joke and story, and often it grows each time it is repeated. You only have to think of fishermen relating the relative size of their catch to each other.

This can be put to use in a game called 'What's The Worst That Can Happen?'

Take a matter that is causing you some concern. It can be trivial or major, current or not.

Imagine the worst possible outcome or scenario. Use fantasy to go beyond the obvious. This is also a great way to exercise expanding your limitations. It sometimes helps to realise that you can laugh at the absurdity of your fears.

Then you can do the same process to find your best possible outcome!

Dissection

This is similar to the exaggeration exercise, but in reverse. By delving into the detail of the matter concerning you it can both become trivial, and at the same time you may gain a deeper understanding of just what it is and why it's bothering you.

INCREASE YOUR PLAY POWER

1. Go outside – unplugged and offline – for at least fifteen minutes a day. Yes, that's without any digital devices!
2. Say 'I love you' to someone every day. It might be to yourself when you look in the mirror, or it may be in a message or a phone call, rather than in person, but make sure that you do it daily.
3. Say 'thank you' to three people every day. You'll soon find that you can increase this, and do it nine times a day. Challenge yourself to up your gratitude attitude!

S.A.L.T. STRATEGY

People all around the world flock to the shores. What's the attraction? At heart it is the salty, tangy freshness. Even if you can't get to the sea every day, you can still give yourself a daily dose of SALT:

S – Stretch – your body, your heart, and your mind! Do yoga, tai chi, chi gong, pilates, or sun salutations. Find your own simple sequence of stretches and add to it. Put on your favourite music if you like. Stretch your imagination to visualise the best you can be.

A – Attitude – is central to how you make your decisions each day. It involves inner thought, and commitment to a particular set of values, or standards. Attitude is revealed in the actions we take, as well as the thoughts and emotions we have. This takes three steps:

Firstly, think about awareness, attention and action. Unless you are first **AWARE** of your situation, there is no real basis for your attitude. This means not only aware of your outer environment, and the intentions of the people around you, but also being aware of your own inner intent. This involves the development of your own value system, from inside out.

Secondly, attitude depends on what you give your **attention** to. Just like a plant you tend, or a project you are working on, what you give your attention to will grow and flourish.

Finally, there is no development without **action** being taken. You must regularly do what needs to be done to attain a goal. This can also mean taking action to secure the support of others who are skilled in areas that you are not. They will supplement your drive, and create a synergy that is bigger than the sum of its parts.

L – L**aughter** – the most efficient way to health and wellbeing. Get informed to understand its awesome power. Know what tickles your funny bone and do it regularly, and make a laughter action plan using the exercises in this book.

T – **Thanks** – gratitude for what you have in life brings everything together. Count your blessings – think of things to be thankful for. Recite these blessings first thing in the morning, at noon and at night. Put the power of praise into practice. Do kind acts! Nurture your 'Attitude of Gratitude.'

GOT A LOT ON YOUR PLATE?

The Balancing Act

With one being the most important, and five being the least important, number each of the life areas and each of the quotients from one to five, relative to how important they are to you.

This will indicate where you may focus on your strengths, and other areas where you could develop yourself.

LIFE AREAS

Friends/Family

Job/Work/Profession

ME

Social/Sports

Wider World

QUOTIENTS

IQ – Intellectual

EQ – Emotional

SQ – Spiritual

PQ – Physical

HQ – Humour

Your Five 'M's. You can remember these on the fingers of one hand. Touch each fingertip to remind yourself each day to action them.

Notice that they have the five vowels, 'Ma.., Me.., Mi.., Mo.., Mu' to make it easier to recall.

Choose and do at least three of these daily. Aim to do all five.

Magic

Find at least one thing every day that fills you with awe and wonder.

With wonder comes inspiration. From inspiration comes courage. And from courage comes action.

Meditation

Take time out for contemplation, prayer or reflection. Do a minimum of ten minutes. Increase this to fifteen or twenty minutes once you have established a routine.

Mission

This 'middle 'M' relates to all the others. Having a mission, a goal or purpose is vital. So take a moment to decide on where you're going. It's not about why or how. Without a direction you're just drifting. Would you leave your house without knowing which way to turn?

An easy way to tell if you have a mission is to look at the actions you take every day. Put simply, do your thoughts and desires align with your actions? And vice versa, do your actions align with your ideas?

Movement

Walk, run, roll, swim, sport, dance, jump, swing, skip, twist, juggle!

There are many ways to move. Choose the one/s that appeal to you!

Music

With the power to move our emotions, music has a magic quality that you can harness. It doesn't matter what style, if you enjoy it make sure you have it in your life! Remember those songs that have special meaning for you. Learn the words or try listening to something new.

Here's some extra M's to mix in, and of course add any of your own:

Meeting: One or more people, preferably face to face.

Massage: Decide who will give and who will receive. A massage doesn't have to involve oils or hot stones. It can be as simple as making contact, e.g. holding hands.

A hug is a massage. Eight hugs per day is the recommended minimum. Make them as extended as possible – twenty seconds is the optimal duration to generate real results! Reach out to touch... Even extended eye contact is extremely intimate. Connect; don't rush.

If you do not have anyone to share physical contact with, you can always contact someone online or by phone.

Laugh

Thanks to the dedication of the wonderful couple, Dr Madan Kataria and Madhuri Kataria, Laughter Yoga has spread steadily since its beginnings in 1995.

The beauty of this simple system is that anyone can do it, anywhere and anytime. There are no prerequisites. A group of laughers can be set up with minimal requirements. Nothing more is required than a time, a place, and the willingness of participants to laugh together.

Laughter Yoga can also be done solo, just like any other yoga or fitness regime. But it's easier and more fun in a group.

There are many resources available for anyone wishing to learn how to practice Laughter Yoga, from DVD's, books, and CD's. to whole training courses, which are available online.

It helps if there are other people to share your laughter with. The best scenario is a core group of people with experience to get the club started and to keep it going.

They can either be trained in the leadership courses or make the effort to study the methods and immerse themselves in established laughter groups long enough to gain the required experience and skills of leadership.

Dr Kataria and his wife toured extensively for over ten years to take Laughter Yoga into as many countries as were open to the concept. Sometimes it was a school, a business, or an individual who invited them into a new land. With focussed dedication they travelled for many months of the year, leaving in their wake a trail of living laughter clubs.

Laughter clubs now exist in over one hundred countries around the planet. In some countries there is just one small club. In others, like India and America, there are literally thousands.

The beautiful thing is, along with a common set of laughs that are shared in all clubs worldwide, each country invents and develops their very own laughs. These laughs are sometimes characteristic of their country of origin.

For example, in Australia we have the 'Kookaburra Laugh'; and in England the 'One-Metre Laugh' from India became the 'Robin Hood Laugh'. In Eastern Europe one man decided that laughter is the ideal antidote to a tradition there enforcing a cult of seriousness on their culture.

Every country across Europe has many groups, and there are even some schools of laughter, such as the Ecole de Rire in Paris. On the Spanish island of Tenerife Emilio is collecting laughs from all around the world, as do I, and we share these with groups, both large and small.

Lotte in Paris shared the 'Golf Player Laugh', and the 'LiveRadioStudio Host Laugh' – have you ever noticed how radio presenters always laugh in a particular way when they tell jokes? Well, that's the one. From Germany Vivi and Ulla came up with the 'Mad Cow Laugh', the 'Smoking Laugh' and the 'Ester Williams' Laugh.

At our annual Laughter Yoga conference we have participants from all over Asia as well as around Australia. They come from many places, including Indonesia, South Korea, Japan, and Malaysia.

In Africa, where people face everyday challenges for basic amenities, there are laughter groups. We might imagine that in the Middle East they have too many pressing issues to think about Laughter Yoga. But it is precisely in these places that Laughter Yoga can be most effective, by giving participants the ability to gain balance with conflict raging around them, and insight and strength to nurture themselves and to support others.

In India, the birthplace of Laughter Yoga, there are dozens of clubs in every large city across the country. People meet daily instead of weekly, as is common in Western countries. What is marvellous are the changes that Laughter Yoga has created.

For example, in Laughter Yoga groups people from all castes mix freely. Before Laughter Yoga, women could not be seen laughing in public; opening their mouths to do this was regarded as indecent. There are still vestiges of this in other cultures, e.g. when people cover their mouths in public when eating or laughing.

I get daily inspirations from laughter buddies around the world. That's the beauty of this network, you can invite all those people whom you wish to share a laugh with!

We now have an international body comprised of Master Trainers who have developed standardised training material for use by all qualified leaders and trainers.

A Laughter Story

Kris was shy, so he went to a monthly laughter group. This wasn't enough when he got the bug, so he looked for a group where he could go weekly, and then daily! For eight days straight he laughed on a laughter boat in Belgium, until he was not as shy as he was before.

Over the twenty years that I have been running laughter clubs I have heard so many wonderful stories like this. This playful, joyful silliness is also a spiritual experience. After all, the origin of the word 'silly' is from the Germanic 'selig', meaning holy.

Focusing on the breath, and connecting our inside with the outside is as good as it gets. The fact that we do this in a fun, easy way with a group doesn't diminish our dedication to health and fitness. Laughter Yoga tones up every bodily system. And cultivating a healthy body ain't a bad way to start the day!

SEVEN CHAKRAS LAUGHTER – THIRD EYE CHAKRA

For the HEAD we laugh, 'Hee-hee-hee, hi-hi-hi'

The sixth 'Hi-hi-hi' is the laugh of the third eye chakra, just above and between your eyes. The 'hi' is pronounced 'high.'

Rainbow Laughter Rites – Indigo

Breathe and settle into your quiet place. Feel your head open at the top and lavender scented energy enter. See the colour and welcome it through you and down to your HOME. Laugh with joy, and end with peaceful breaths.

'Beneath the mountain the stream flows on and on without end. If one's Zen mind is like this, seeing into one's nature cannot be far off.'
— Hakuin, Japanese Zen Buddhist (1686–1768)

7 ROLL ON!

'To see a world in a grain of sand and a heaven in a wild flower, hold infinity in the palm of your hand and eternity in an hour'

— William Blake (1757–1827)

In this chapter the focus is on consolidating everything you have learned throughout this book.

The Japanese have a saying that the last 5% of a task is really half the job. Often, it's at that point that so many people give in and drop out.

This is when 'grit' is needed. By now, you have integrated the three parts of yourself, your head, heart and home. Through regular breath, play, and laughter activities they become one integral whole. You have integrity!

With constant practice it makes the continuation easier when you are required to perform under pressure. You know how to access that final 5%!

As we saw earlier, we can also apply our 80/20 power ratio here. So with 80% of the work done, you've only used 20% of your energy. You need to dig deep to get that last 20% finished, because it will call on a massive 80% of your resources!

BREATHE

By gaining a greater ability to breathe into your centre, you become aware of your inner core. This increased familiarity with both your body and your essential 'being' will also increase your feelings of self-worth and self-love.

This works on both the macro and micro levels equally. When we feel great overall, then every cell of our body sings along.

Rainbow Breathing Rites – Violet

Altruistic Breathing: eyes closed, breathe for someone else, preferably someone you don't like. Imagine you are that person, and each breath you take brings them strength, peace, healing.

Aim for three minutes, or about twenty breaths, to start with. You will soon extend this to twenty minutes when you add some MindMT techniques.

All Seven Rainbow Breathing Rites Together

Red – Basic breathing: bringing your awareness to the breath, both the in and out breaths, as well as the moments of change between the breaths. Do not 'control' these, simply become aware of the process.

Orange – Dawn Breathing: take a deep inhalation and make a big smile as you open imaginary curtains to a new day. Let the sun shine in. Rejoice at what you see. Laugh out loud – as:.............. Then open another imaginary window and repeat. Do this a few times. SG adapted

Yellow – Out Breathing: breathe out longer than you breathe in.

Green – Awareness Breathing: encounter a moment of beauty every day. Stop, take three breaths to settle, and then count ten breaths while focusing on the beauty before you. You will not only become more aware of the detail, you become more aware of your body.

Blue – Wave Breathing: like the waves lap into the shore and roll out again, our breaths have their own natural rhythm.

Indigo – Nose Breathing: holding one nostril at a time, with either forefinger or thumb.

Violet – Altruistic Breathing: eyes closed, breathe for someone else, preferably someone you don't like. Imagine you are that person, and each breath you take brings them strength, peace, healing.

PLAY

Letting Go Means Falling

One of our biggest blocks to letting ourselves play is our fear of failure.

This combines with some of our other common fears: that of being embarrassed by looking silly in public, and also a fear of asking questions and appearing stupid.

Play is experimenting, and by definition this means that there are going to be blind alleys, red herrings, and frustrating false leads. The stigma of failure is so strong that we avoid anything that may lead us up that path.

But in real life it's about problem-solving. A situation arises and we have to deal with it, right now. And we don't always have the right answer!

As the saying goes, the ability to make right decisions comes from experience. But how do you get experience? By making wrong decisions! So it's all about perspective. If you want to call them mistakes, they will be. But if they are learning experiences, if they are seen as new challenges, they take on a different meaning.

As Thomas Edison said, 'I have not failed 500 times, I have successfully found 500 ways that it will not work.' In some quotes the number is Edison said was 10,000 times!

The failure is not in falling, but in staying down and not getting up again.

Play Magic

Another block to play is that we are often unsure where it will lead. Most people like to know their destination before they set out. It makes sense that if we leave the house to go somewhere, we check the directions first so that we know which way to turn out of the driveway! But even when they accept the invitation to play, they really want it to be a comfortable, easy ride.

They want clear parameters, and full risk management. With play, there are no guarantees that it's safe, or that it will be a good use of time. Opening up to 'anything goes' is too scary for some people.

Like Pandora's box, once it is open we fear that we may be releasing forces beyond our control. But therein lies the magic.

Despite people now knowing that magic is a mixture of highly skilled technique with some scientific assistance, they still come and enjoy a good magician.

The reason why magicians practice for so long is not only to entertain us. It is to provide a metaphor for something much bigger and deeper. They play with our minds precisely to 're-mind' us that things are not always as they seem. Their unspoken message is that there are many ways to perceive something, and also that altering our perception can be fun.

A professor of psychology at the University of Hertfordshire, England, did an experiment where he had magic tricks taught in the classroom of a school.

It was found that the increase in the students' self-esteem was more than in a control class of 'normal' self-esteem.

As you can imagine, the students wanted to do more magic, but they were also eager to learn more in all their subjects, and were more likely to be self-starters and to develop discipline.

Play Paralysis

Play Paralysis is when people are afraid of letting themselves play. They can't loosen up inside and enjoy the things that happen during their day.

Understanding yourself is the key to life-balance and personal wellbeing. And the first step is awareness – of what's inside you, and how you connect what's inside with what's outside.

When you get an idea and decide to act on it, the choice has often only been made in your head. Yet when you take action on a decision, you need the head, the heart, and the home to agree! Unless all three are on board, there will be misalignment and disconnection. You need to learn to listen to yourself.

How? You follow your deepest needs first. You learn to listen to your 'gut feeling', and then things can be run past the head and the heart.

Every decision you make, big or small, is the same process.

The way you do anything is the way you do everything. This is called fractal theory, or the 'butterfly effect.' Every little action or thought is a template for the big ones.

This means that you can train your brain with every choice you make, by checking in with your heart and body when making even relatively small decisions.

In practice, you often let your emotions take over and sway you.[31] For example, when the sun is shining it is easy to say, 'I'll leave a job until later, and go out to enjoy the sunshine.'

When some extra dessert is on offer, you can't think of any reason not to indulge. Why not? Well, because you don't really think at all.

It is in these tiny ways that you can prepare your ability to make the bigger decisions. If you do decide to indulge yourself, accept and enjoy it to the full. Otherwise, the worry over it will do you more harm than the extra fat and sugar ever could!

Home

Your body is your home. It is where your centre of balance and your life force reside. It's also the home of your values, which create meaning in your life. It is the first authority, even before the head. Your home should be the base of who you are, to form a solid foundation for the rest.

> 'The two most important days in your life are the day that you are born and the day you find out why.' — Mark Twain

HOW TO JUMP FOR JOY!

The Four Pillars of Joy

Do you remember the four pillars of joy? They are song, dance, laughter and play. You now have a wide variety of ways to keep these as permanent, integrated threads in your life.

Here are some additonal ways to look at joy that I'd love to share.

The Five Characteristics of Joy

Ingrid Fetell Lee is a designer who studied joy – specifically, what it is that makes us joyful. She found that there are five common traits to joy.

1. Things with circular or round shapes. Objects with curves are more readily accepted by us than sharp, angular ones. A study by neuroscientists showed that our brains prefer the former over the latter. This is due to the fact that angular objects can be dangerous. This could also have something to do with our familiarity with the human form.
2. Bright colours. This seems obvious, yet we do need reminding that this stems from nature's ability to show off. Bright colours are a sign of life force and energy.
3. High, ascending lines and objects that take our eyes skywards. We only have to think of a balloon taking off (brightly coloured and circular), or a bird in flight.
4. Abundance is also a characteristic of joy. In nature, it signals survival. The opposite – a lack of resources – means deprivation.
5. Patterns are more pleasing than chaotic designs.

Whenever we put several of these 'characteristics' of joy together, we create the environment for a joyful experience. That is, we set up the situation to suit ourselves, rather than relying on chance.

Publicolor is a group that paints schools in big, bold rainbow colour patterns. School administrators reported that:

- attendance improves;
- graffiti disappears, and;
- kids say they feel safer.

This aligns with research in four countries showing that people working in colourful offices are:

- more alert;
- more confident, and;
- friendlier.

Use Joy as a Verb!

Joy, like breathe, play and laugh, can be both a noun and a verb. When you experience joy, you rejoice! By allowing yourself to rejoice you feel wholly present in yourself as well as in your world.

To start with you'll probably want to focus on each laugh, and then the sequence. This is easiest to do when sitting or standing, however you feel most comfortable.

Once I established this whole sequence, I found I enjoy doing this set of Chakra laughs in a variety of ways. For example when I'm out walking, or doing daily chores.

I even add a movement to each laugh, to make it a combination exercise. But this was only after long repetition, many months of doing each stage. So if you feel it's fun to add some movement, fine. But don't be in any hurry!

Seven Chakras Laughter – From Root To Crown

For the HOME we laugh, 'Hoo-hoo-hoo, Ho-ho-ho.' The 'hoo' is pronounced like an owl's 'who'. The 'ho' is pronounced 'hoe', like Santa's 'ho'.

For the HEART we laugh, 'Ha-ha-ha, Hey-hey-hey.' The 'ha' is our 'normal' laugh. The 'hey' is pronounced 'hay'.

For the HEAD we laugh, 'Hee-hee-hee, hi-hi-hi.' The 'hi' is pronounced 'high.'

These laughs align with the seven chakras, or our 'energy nodes'.

The first 'Hoo-hoo-hoo' is the laugh of the root chakra, at the junction of your legs.

The second 'Ho-ho-ho' is the laugh of the sacral chakra, just below your navel.

The third 'Ha-ha-ha' is the laugh of the solar-plexus chakra, at the base of your ribcage.

The fourth 'Hey-hey-hey' is the laugh of the heart chakra, in the centre of your chest.

The fifth 'Hee-hee-hee' is the laugh of the throat chakra, which is found on your neck.

The sixth 'Hi-hi-hi' is the laugh of the third eye chakra, just above and between your eyes.

The final seventh laugh is silent, and is the laugh of the crown chakra. It goes from the top of the head and loops back to the bottom. This is a chance to focus only on the breath, with minimal or without any sound.

Tips

This may seem a lot to remember, so begin by doing just one at a time. Simply add another one when you feel ready.

You do not need to get the laugh 'exactly' on the chakra points at this stage. That can come later, when you are comfortable with the combination.

Once you are clear on these you can proceed to do them in order – from the bottom up!

You do not need to get all seven laughs in one breath. Go as far as you can with each breath.

Focus on the area for each of the laughs, and then flow to the next chakra. You can take another breath whenever you need.

Eventually, you may find it fun to get all the seven laughs into one breath.

Variation

I recommend that you have a go at doing each laugh three times, rather than twice. That is, 'Hoo-hoo-hoo.' I find that this helps with the flow, by taking your mind away from the regular two-beat rhythm. Perhaps there is something about the '¾ beat', which we associate with dancing.

If this doesn't feel comfortable then you are welcome to stick with two, or try four laughs. It's all about feeling the fun in the laughter.

Rainbow Laughter Rites – Violet

Picture a field of lovely violet flowers waving in the sunshine. Hedges of rosemary line the field.

Enter through a gap in the hedge and take in their perfume as you breathe in, laughing as you breathe out!

Skip or walk around the field taking three big breaths and laughing, then exit through the gap in the hedge and out into the world again.

Last Laughs!

Feel The Laughter Vibrations – Laugh out loud while putting your hands on your hips, belly/abdomen, diaphragm, chest, throat and head – forehead then to top & 'hum' – to feel the vibrations that different laughter sounds make.

Memories – 'Seeing Eye' Laugh – Close your eyes and take a couple of deep breaths as you go back in time looking for a happy memory. When you have it, smile now as if you were back then.

'The quieter you become the more you are able to hear.'

– Zen saying

CONCLUSION

'Stop acting so small. You are the universe in ecstatic motion.' — Rumi

WHAT'S YOUR PURPOSE?

Michael J. is an American comedian and also a motivational/ inspirational speaker. He is funny, delivering a string of jokes with a relaxed style.

Then he explains how a joke works: the first part, the 'setup,' followed by the punchline. As we know, any joke needs both parts to create the desired result, laughter.

The end effect is brought about by a twist, a change from the setup. Rather than the expected result suggested by the setup, there is a new surprise element introduced in the punchline.

Here's a very short example: 'Six out of seven dwarves are not Happy.'

That's only eight words, but there's still a setup and a punchline.

When you read or hear the words 'seven dwarves', your mind immediately associates this with the well-known story of Snow White and the Seven Dwarves.

You know that they all have individual names, although you may not remember them all. And then the punchline comes by simply stating the obvious.

There is an element of truth in all good comedy, and this joke works because it literally tells the truth. You also do the mental leap of realising that it's not so much about the numbers as the names. So the surprise switch works on several levels at once.

After Michael J. explains how humour works, he makes what I consider to be a very powerful point for our lives. He likens the setup of a joke to all that we do in our daily lives – establishing ourselves in a job, a place to live, relationships, etc. All the stuff that we call life and consider so important, he calls this just the setup.

So what is your punchline, he asks? Why go to all the trouble of doing this set up if there is no purpose? Remember that the setup by its very nature generates expectation.

Without a reason, an aim, or a goal, you are just going to be adding more and more to your 'setup.'

Now that you have empowered yourself to move, you can always set greater goals. Your human nature is designed to rise to any challenge, and draw the required resources together. Be bold and be beautiful!

The Sweet Spot

There is a 'sweet spot' **where the serious and the silly meet**. It is there you can make your home.

By getting out of your head and performing a 'heart bypass,' you bring your awareness down into your solar plexus, your 'home'.

This is not about navel gazing, or sticking your head up where the sun doesn't shine! Remember how you flipped the top pyramid to your bottom bigger one?

This gives your attention to **the vagas nerve**, the direct connector between the bottom and the top of your body. The vagas nerve is the 'super-highway' from your home to your head, linking both of these, all along the way.

It transmits messages directly from your home base, to correct the imbalance of our 'head-heavy' lives. So at this stage you are in an optimal state to connect, communicate and contribute.

By now you should have a better understanding of why you are here. I hope you have discovered how you can give out all the wonderful gifts you have, and how brilliantly you shine when you do this. You now know how to live longer and stronger, and how to breathe, play and laugh louder and longer.

> 'We must always change, renew, rejuvenate ourselves, otherwise we harden.'
> — Johann Von Goethe (1749–1832)

APPENDIX I

7 BREATHS & 7 LAUGHS

> VIOLET: Altruistic Breath: Eyes closed, breathe for someone else, preferably someone you don't like. Imagine you are them, and each breath you take brings them strength, peace, healing...
>
> — by Sebastian Gendry

6. PURPLE: 'Nose Breathing.' Holding one nostril at a time, with either forefinger or thumb.

5. BLUE: 'Wave Breathing.' Like the waves lap into the shore and roll out again, our breaths have their own natural rhythm. Feel your body filling with salt water.

4. GREEN: 'Encounter' every day a moment of beauty. Stop, take three breaths to settle, and then count ten breaths while focusing on the beauty before you. You will not only become more aware of the detail, you become more aware of your body.

There are a whole variety of ways to use this simple technique. Here are a few more suggestions: You can sit and bring to mind your own happy image, and focus on this while doing the ten breaths, and you can also focus the energy to any part of your body which needs it. See: Glen Schneider's, 'Ten Breaths to Happiness.'

3. YELLOW: Out Breathing – breathe out longer than you breathe in.

2. ORANGE: **DAWN Breath:** Take a deep inhalation and smile as you open imaginary curtains to a new day. Let the sun shine in. Rejoice at what you see. Laugh out loud! Then open another imaginary window and repeat. Do this a few times by moving into each 'room' of your house.

At SUNSET take a moment to marvel at the changing light show. Breathe out, letting go of the day's cares. Give thanks for the ups and downs, the ins and outs of your day, just like every breath you take.

1. RED: 'Basic breathing.' Bringing your awareness to the breath, both the in and out breaths, as well as the moments of change between these. Do not 'control' these, simply become aware of the process.

Aim for three minutes, or about twenty breaths to start with. You will soon extend this to twenty minutes when you add some MindMT techniques.

7 LAUGHS

For all 7:

Feel The Laughter Vibrations: Laugh out loud while putting your hands on your hips, belly/abdomen, diaphragm, chest, throat and head – forehead then to top & 'hum' – to feel the vibrations that different laughter sounds make.

7. **PURPLE: 'Seeing eye' Laugh.** Close your eyes and take a couple of deep breaths as you go back in time looking for a happy memory.

When you have it, smile now as if you were back then.

Now turn the smile into a laugh! [**H Memories Chuckle**] **SG**

6. '**Violet' Laughter:** Picture a field of lovely violet flowers waving in the sunshine. Hedges of rosemary line the field. Enter through a gap in the hedge and take in their perfume as you breathe in, laughing as you breathe out!

Skip or walk around the field taking three big breaths and laughing. Then exit through the gap in the hedge and out into the world again.

5. BLUE LAUGHTER

'**Ocean' Laughter:** While laughing, sway from side to side, rocking like a boat on the ocean.

'**Tropical Waterfall' Laughter**: Close your eyes. Laugh as you imagine taking a shower under a warm tropical waterfall.

Avoid Fishing Hooks and Laugh: While laughing, swim around imaginary fishing hooks in the water. This is a great metaphor for learning to avoid life's challenges.

'**Washing Machine' Laugh:**

1. Laugh as you open the door/lift the lid and insert clothes.
2. Switch on the washing machine – press your belly button and laugh!
3. Wash cycle, laugh with a low 'Hoo, Hoo, Ho, Ho.'
4. Rinse cycle – core/heart laughs, 'Ha, Ha...'
5. Spin dry cycle – high 'Hee, Hee!'

4. **GREEN: Heart Expansion Laughter:** Cover your heart with both hands and laugh from soft to loud as you slowly open your arms wider and wider.

Hearty Laughter: Make an elongated "aeeee" sound as you slowly lift both arms all the way up, then laugh heartily with your hands pointed to the sky. Imagine that your laughter is coming straight from your heart.

Healing/Body Scan Laughter: Be aware of any aches, discomforts or itches that you have – don't push them away, just be aware. Laugh from that area of pain or itch and imagine that some of the discomfort is exhaled with the laughter, leaving your body.

3. YELLOW: **Banana Laughter**: Smile as you peel a banana and look forward to enjoying every bite. Suddenly a monkey grabs your banana and runs away! Laugh as you get up and chase him!

Sunshine Laughter: Fling the curtains open and laugh as the sun streams in. Do this to each room in the house.

2. ORANGE: Pick oranges from a tree with laughter. Pop them in your bag or basket. Peel and smell the oranges with laughter.

Juice them by twisting your wrists – swap hands to use both sides.

Imagine you are watching a sunset, breathing deep and sighing at the beauty. You can make a ring for the sun with one hand's fingers, and a horizon with the other arm. Let the sun slowly sink, and laugh as you imagine vivid orange colours lighting up the sky. Better still, go out at that time and watch the real thing, laughing at the glory of this change from day to night.

SANTA LAUGHTER: Hold your belly and give the deepest 'goodwill to all' 'Ho-ho-ho! laugh as you can as Santa.

Big Friendly Giant LAUGHTER: Be the tallest giant you can be and give a friendly, rumbling laugh that reverberates far and wide. You can mix in a few 'Fi-fie-fo-fums' for fun as a scary variation if you like, then finish with the friendly giant laugh again.

1. RED:

Make A Fire: Laugh as you mime making fire without matches, by creating sparks with flint stones, or rubbing a stick between your hands like a drill.

Hot Coals Laughter: Walk on red-hot coals, breathing sharp, short breaths as you keep moving and get to the other side!

Red Light Laugh: Laugh like your car engine as you drive along the road with a steady, 'internal' laugh. A 'Red light' ahead and you have to stop! Laugh out loud at your going nowhere. 'Green Light!' and you take off again. You meet two more red lights and you're there, so get out and get going!

APPENDIX 2

THE WELLNESS ALPHABET

A 'BONUS' STRATEGY – A VISUAL REMINDER TO KEEP YOU ON TRACK ALONG THE WELLNESS PATH TO YOUR HAPPINESS HOUSE EACH DAY.

Your TETRAHEDRON to make is included inside the back cover.

This can be used in various ways. Here are three suggestions.

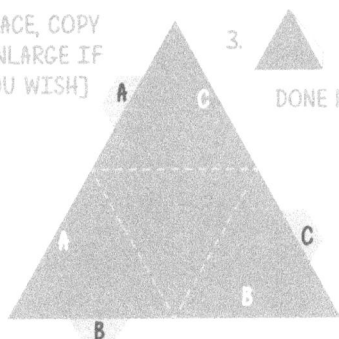

YOUR TETRAHEDRON TEMPLATE
TO COLOUR IN!

A.

1. Firstly, you choose four words from the 'Wellbeing Alphabet' list that you feel have meaning for you. Don't think too much about them, take those that feel right for you now. There's plenty to choose from.
2. Now write, or attach these words on the faces of the four triangles. [e.g. there are mini-sticky notes available].

With words on each of the four 'faces,' three faces form the sides of the pyramid, and one face will always be out of sight on the base. Also, only one face is visible at a time. They will change as you turn the tetrahedron, to choose which to view.

The figure can be turned as you wish. Each side is available, and no one corner need remain at the 'top'. It is for you to decide which way this is to be set at any time.

This may depend on your mood, the circumstances of your day, and many other factors. Or you can turn it at regular intervals, to have fresh reminders of the 'power' or 'inspiration' words that you have selected as important for you.

You can change the words as often as you like. Choose from the other suggested words, and substitute them. Remember, these are just suggestions.

You may have your own words with special meaning for you.

[Note that the tetrahedron also has four corners, or tips. The tetrahedron shape means that one tip is always at the apex or top, and the other three form the 'base' for the pyramid.]

B.

Secondly, you can make four words into a sentence. This can be your mantra, or affirmation. It's a great feeling to say it out loud regularly.

Write yours down on the faces of the tetrahedron, and keep it in a prominent place.

C.

The tetrahedron allows you to focus on one panel at once.

You can use this for example to plan a project, or your jobs for the day.

Put the four dot points or elements of your plan on the four spaces and start with your first step. Its 3D nature means you can set it where only one side is visible at a time.

You can of course make multiple copies of this tetrahedron. Decide whether you wish to re-use, recycle them or destroy them.

THE WELLNESS ALPHABET

A – Attitude Attention Awareness Action Alignment Ally Ambition

Aspire Attain Awe

Authority Absolve Absolute Abundance Accept Accountable

Affirmative Agape

Air Amaze Ample Atone Available

B – BREATHE Balance Be Belief Breath Beauty Best Become

Begin Being Body Bold

Bond Boost Bounty Bubble Build

C – Commitment Clarity Consistency

Care Courage Curious Core

Control/Chaos Continue Connect/Communicate

D – Decide Discover Dance Dare Do Dream Delight Drive Dignity

Diligence Direction Draw Duty Deference Degree Determination

Discernment Discuss Discriminate Distinguish Disposal Divine

Drama Devotion

Discretion Delegate Doubt Deal Dopamine Death Define Defend

Design Deity Deliberate Deliver Dependable Depth Derivation

E– Ease Effective Education Enjoy Effluence Efficient Economical

Energy Eager

Earnest Excel Express Earn Earth Easy Effort Element Empathy

Engage

Environment Essence Ethic

F – Fun Food Fitness Feeling Free Flexibility

Fountain Fat Fresh Fast Forgive Face

Factor Fair Faith Fail Family Fate

Fire Flow Flower Folk For Form Firm Fancy

G – Gratitude Genius Guide Gentle Game

Generate Generous Genesis Gift

Give Go Good Grant Grow Garlic Ginger Ginko

H – Heart (Helping) Happiness Health

Humour Harmony Holy

Home Human Humble

I – Intuition Intention Idea Integrity Instinct

Identity Infinite Impulse Impossible

Increase If Ignorance- 'we are all ignorant about something'

Instant Ineffable Instrument Ignite

Immune Impact Impart Impress Improve

Inalienable Incisive Include Independent

Intense Interest Inner/Intentional Intimacy Intonation

Intrinsic Issue Irony

J – Joy Join Journey Just Jump Jungle Juggle

Joker Jester Jewel Jolt Jog

Judge Juice Juxtapose

K – Key Kind Know Kernel Knack Kit

Kaleidoscope Karma Keep Kin King

L – LAUGH/ter Love Life Lever/age Last Lemon
Level Lateral Latent Law/Lore
Luck Lead Learn Leisure Let Light Loyal
Live Lesson Less Lack

M – Movement Meditation Music Magic Massage
Miracle Merlot Metaphor
Manifest Manage Magnetic Mantra Map Mind Meet Mirth
Moderate Motive Myth Mutual Mask

N – Nature Name Now Need Namaste Nourish
Nothingness Nutrition Notion Nose
Notice New Nest Nascent Native Narrate

O – On One Open Opportunity Offer
Original Order Out Own

P – PLAY Passion Persistence Perseverance Patience
Pleasure Perfect Praise

Q – Quest Query/Quiz Quotient Quota Queen

R – Recognise Resolve Release Resilience
Respite Response Rest Rise

S – Sacred Sacrifice Safe Sage Saint Sanctuary
Satisfy Save Science Search Seek See

Seed Self Sense Serve Settle Sex Shadow Share

Shine Shift Sing Smile Social

Spine Sign Silence Simplify Spiral Spirit Sport Spring Strength

Substantial Symmetry System

Synthesis Symbol Succeed Sun Sure Stress Salt Sugar Shalom

T – Trust Target Thanks Transcend Treasure

Tribe Trigger Triumph Table Truth Tact Travel Treat

Take Talk Touch Tongue Tangent Tangible Turn Tune

Tao Tap Task Taste Tenacious Tender Theatre

Team Teach Telepathy Tell Temperance Temple

Theory Thrive time Tithe Tone Tonic Trade Trace Tube

Trance Trait Train Transcend Transform Transmit

U – Ur Ultra Unique Unity Unknown Utility Ukelele

Ultimate Umbra Umbilical Unanimous Undaunted

Undulating Universe Urge Use Utter

V – Value Vision Virtue Volition Valid Vital Variable Vagus

Vigour Valence Valour Vantage Volunteer Voyage

Vapour Vocal Voice Vivacity Void Vacuum Voluntary

Vacation Valediction Vegetables Vector Vent Venture Veracity

Versatile Vehicle Vibration Village Visualise

W – Will Wonder Well Whole Wild With Worth

Wish Walk Wander Want Waltz

Watch Water Wave Way Wind Wood Work

Write World Worship Wealth Whistle Wheel Whim

X – Xcellence Xquisite Xcite Xpert Xtreme Xact

Xylophone Xmas X ray X-Chromosome (2F 1M)

Y – Yes Yield Yoga (yoking; couple) Y–Why?

Yen Youth/Young Yin Yang

Z – Zeal Zest Zone Zero

Zen Zeit-Geist Zenith Zodiac

Zygote (the developing individual)

APPENDIX 3

QUOTES ON MEDITATION

'Sit quietly doing nothing, spring comes, and the grass grows by itself.'
— Zen wisdom.

'Whether moving or standing quiet, the essence of zen is always at ease.'
— Daishi, Japanese monk 774–835

'Alone with yourself, never weary, on the edge of the forest live joyfully, without desire.'
— Buddha

'Each soul must meet the morning sun, the new sweet earth, and the great silence alone!'
— Charles Alexander Eastmann, native American 1858–1939

'When I begin to sit with the dawn in solitude, I begin to really live. It makes me treasure every single moment of life.'
— Gloria Vanderbilt 1924

'If our nature is permitted to guide our life, we grow healthy, fruitful & happy.'
— Abraham Maslow, American psychologist 1908–1970

'The most valuable thing we can do for the psyche, occasionally, is to let it rest, wander, not to be or do anything whatever.'
— May Sarton, 1912–1951

'The real voyage of discovery consists not in seeking new landscapes but in having new eyes.' — Marcel Proust 1871–1922

'It is a common belief that we breathe with our lungs alone, but in point of fact, the work of breathing is done by the whole body. The lungs play a passive role in the respiratory process. Their expansion is produced by an enlargement, mostly downward, of the thoracic cavity and they collapse when that cavity is reduced. Proper breathing involves the muscles of the head, neck, thorax, and abdomen. It can be shown that chronic tension in any part of the body's musculature interferes with the natural respiratory movements.

Breathing is a rhythmic activity. Normally a person at rest makes approximately 16 to 17 respiratory incursions a minute. The rate is higher in infants and in states of excitation. It is lower in sleep and in depressed persons. The depth of the respiratory wave is another factor which varies with emotional states. Breathing becomes shallow when we are frightened or anxious. It deepens with relaxation, pleasure and sleep. But above all, it is the quality of the respiratory movements that determines whether breathing is pleasurable or not. With each breath a wave can be seen to ascend and descend through the body. The inspiratory wave begins deep in the abdomen with a backward movement of the pelvis. This allows the belly to expand outward. The wave then moves upward as the rest of the body expands. The head moves very slightly forward to suck in the air while the nostrils dilate or the mouth opens. The expiratory wave begins in the upper part of the body and moves downward: the head drops back, the chest and abdomen collapse, and the pelvis rocks forward.

Breathing easily and fully is one of the basic pleasures of being alive. The pleasure is clearly experienced at the end of expiration when the descending wave fills the pelvis with a delicious sensation. In adults this sensation has a sexual quality, though it does not induce any genital feeling. The slight backward and forward movements of the pelvis, similar to the sexual movements, add to the pleasure. Though the rhythm of breathing is pronounced in the pelvic area, it is at the same time experienced by the total body as a feeling of fluidity, softness, lightness and excitement.

The importance of breathing need hardly be stressed. It provides the oxygen for the metabolic processes; literally it supports the fires of life. But breath as "pneuma" is also the spirit or soul. We live in an ocean of air like fish in a body of water. By our breathing we are attuned to our atmosphere. If we inhibit our breathing we isolate ourselves from the medium in which we exist. In all Oriental and mystic philosophies, the breath holds the secret to the highest bliss. That is why breathing is the dominant factor in the practice of Yoga.'
—Alexander Lowen, The Voice of the Body

QUOTES ON BREATH

Oxygen
'Everything needs it: bone, muscles, and even,
while it calls the earth its home, the soul.
So the merciful, noisy machine

stands in our house working away in its
lung-like voice. I hear it as I kneel
before the fire, stirring with a

stick of iron, letting the logs
lie more loosely. You, in the upstairs room,
are in your usual position, leaning on your

right shoulder which aches
all day. You are breathing
patiently; it is a

beautiful sound. It is
your life, which is so close
to my own that I would not know

where to drop the knife of
separation. And what does this have to do
with love, except

everything? Now the fire rises
and offers a dozen, singing, deep-red
roses of flame. Then it settles

to quietude, or maybe gratitude, as it feeds
as we all do, as we must, upon the invisible gift:
our purest, sweet necessity: the air.'
— Mary Oliver, *Thirst*

'Breathing involves a continual oscillation between exhaling and inhaling,
offering ourselves to the world at one moment and drawing the world into
ourselves at the next...'
—David Abram, *Becoming Animal: An Earthly Cosmology*

'Divide the constant tide and random noisiness of energetic flow, with conscious
recurring moments of empty mind, solitude, gratitude and deep...slow...breathing.
Of this, the natural law of self-preservation demands.' — T.F. Hodge, From
Within I Rise: Spiritual Triumph Over Death and Conscious Encounters with
"The Divine Presence"'

'We too should make ourselves empty, that the great soul of the universe
may fill us with its breath.' — Laurence Binyon [SEE ALSO BOOKS ON
CHINA/ART]

Sometimes it all becomes too much. Your body and mind will just give way.
Part of you may want to blissfully fade into nothing, but you never do. After
a while all the memories and emotions make you shut down but never fully
disappear—it's safer for you this way, to be excluded. It's a time to be alone,

to heal, and to find yourself. It doesn't mean you've given up or stopped trying; it just means you know what's best for you.'

QUOTES ON PLAY

'We are all infant prodigies' — Thomas Mann

'In terms of game theory, we might say the universe is so constituted as to maximize the play' — John Leonard

'Life must be lived as play' — Plato

'Lest ye become as little children, ye shall not enter the Kingdom of Heaven' — The Bible

'Culture arises in and as play' — Johan Huizinga.

'Come live and be merry and you join with me, to sing the sweet chorus of Ha-Ha-Hee!' — William Blake

'Body & spirit are twins. God only knows which is which.' — Swinburne

'I give my first hour to god, and god gives me the rest.' — Martin Luther King, when asked by a journalist how he achieved so much in each day.

'The secret of change is to focus all of your energy, not on fighting the old, but on building the new.' — Socrates

'When one completes the journey to one's own heart, one will find oneself in the heart of everyone else.' — Father Thomas Keating

'The intuitive mind is a sacred gift and the rational mind is a faithful servant. We have created a society that honors the servant and has forgotten the gift.' — Albert Einstein

'Trying to be happy by accumulating possessions is like trying to satisfy hunger by taping sandwiches all over your body.' — George Carlin

'Tell me, I forget. Show me, I remember. Involve me, I understand.' — Chinese Proverb

'Remember that your natural state is joy.' — Wayne Dyer

'The first fifty years of childhood are the toughest.' — Anon

'You need chaos in your soul to give birth to a dancing star.' — Friedrich Nietzsche

'There is no such thing as 'Age Appropriate' when it comes to play. At every age play is not a luxury; play is a necessity.

When a three year old asks you to get in her tent, you get in the tent!

Life is play that does not allow testing. So sing, cry, dance, laugh and live intensely. Before the curtain is closed and the piece ends with no applause.' — Charlie Chaplin

'We let our natural self guide us, and we enjoy being who we really are.' — Dr. Kataria

'Play is the highest form of research.' — Albert Einstein

'Let it go, Let it out, Let it all unravel, Let it free and it will be a path on which to travel.' — Michael Leunig

'The body heals with play, the mind heals with laughter, and the soul heals with joy.' — Yiddish Proverb

"Our deepest fear is not that we are inadequate. Our deepest fear
is that we are powerful beyond measure...'Stop Your playing small
doesn't serve the world...
We are born to manifest the glory that is within us.
It's not just within some of us; it's in everyone! As we're liberated from
our own fear, our presence automatically liberates others."

— Marianne Williamson, 1992
(This passage is often incorrectly attributed to Nelson Mandela).

QUOTES ON LAUGHTER & TEARS

'I laugh because I must not cry-
That's all, that's all.'
— Abraham Lincoln

'We look before and after,
And pine for what is not;
Our sincerest laughter
With some pain is fraught;
Our sweetest songs are those
that tell of saddest thought'
— Percy Bysshe Shelley

'Laughs are as honorable as tears. Laughter
and tears are both responses to frustration and
exhaustion, to the futility of thinking and striving
anymore. I myself prefer to laugh, since there is
less cleaning up to do afterward – and since I can
start thinking and striving again that much sooner.'
— Kurt Vonnegut, Jr.

If you have no tragedy, you have no comedy.

'Crying and laughing are the same emotion. If you
laugh too hard, you cry. And vice versa.'
— Sid Caesar

'I never saw anything funny that wasn't terrible.'
— W.C. Fields

'Even in laughter the heart is sorrowful.'
— Proverbs 14: 13

'They laugh often with tears in their eyes.'
— W.C. Fields

'I always knew looking back on my tears
would bring me laughter. But I never knew that
looking back on my laughter would make me cry.'
— Cat Stevens

LAUGHTER & HUMOUR

'If I get big laughs, I'm a comedian. If I get little laughs,
I'm a humorist. If I get no laughs, I'm a singer.'
— George Burns

'A sense of humour is one thing no one will admit to not having.'
— Mark Twain

'Analysing humor is like dissecting a frog. Few
people are interested and the frog dies of it.'
— E.B.White

'Defining and analysing humor is a pastime of humorless people.'
— Robert Benchley

LAUGHTER

'Genuine laughing is the vent of the soul, the
nostrils of the heart, and it is just as necessary for
health and happiness as spring water is for a trout.'
— Josh Billings

'Seven days without laughter makes one weak.'
— Joel Goodman

'Laughter moveth much aire in the breast, and
sendeth the warmer spirits outward.'
— Richard Mulcaster

'Laughter is the sensation of feeling good all over,
and showing it principally in one place.'
— Josh Billings

HUMOUR & JOKES

'I love such mirth as does not make friends
ashamed to look upon one another next morning.'
— Isaak Walton

'Ridicule is just one phase of humor and is not
always the basis for a laugh, although it's a sure-
fire short cut. In ridicule, too, all those who laugh
are not necessarily amused. Sympathy may be
aroused for the poor fellow who is the object of ridicule.'
— Mae West

'Everything is funny as long as it is happening to
somebody else.'
— Will Rogers

'The real wit tells jokes to make others feel
superior, while the half-wit tells them to make
others feel small.'
— Elmer Wheeler

'A jest's prosperity lies in the ear of him that hears
it, never in the tongue of him that makes it.'
— William Shakespeare

'Jests that slap the face are not good jests.'
— Cervantes

LAUGHING AT YOURSELF

'You can't hold a man down without staying down with him.'
— Booker T. Washington

'All of us have schnozzles – are ridiculous in one
way or another, if not in our faces, then in our
characters, minds or habits. When we admit our
schnozzles, instead of defending them, we begin to
laugh, and the world laughs with us.'
— Jimmy Durante

'It dawned on me then that as long as I could
laugh, I was safe from the world; and I have
learned since that laughter keeps me safe from
myself, too.'
— Jimmy Durante

GENERAL

'If a man insisted always on being serious,
and never allowed himself a bit of fun and relaxation,
he would go mad or become unstable without knowing it.'
— Herodotus 484BC–430BC

'Keep away from the wisdom that does not cry, the
philosophy that does not laugh and the greatness
that does not bow before children.'
— Kahlil Gibran

'Fling but a stone, the giant dies. Laugh and be well.'
— Matthew Green

'To whom should I go for some Self-Help? I'm not
always depressed: only when I think or when I feel.'
— Ashley Brilliant

Hilarity Brings Clarity.

APPENDIX 4

QUESTIONNAIRE

How would you classify your type of humour?

Pick as many as apply to you!

Satirical

Sarcastic

Surreal

Playful

Ironic

Imitative

Farcical

Witty

1. **To appreciate the uniqueness of your humour**

   a) When do you find yourself smiling/laughing?

   b) What is it like for you to laugh?

   c) Has humour always been important to you? And for your family?

   d) What shape/style did it take?

   e) Was it always there, or did it develop?

2. About others – community building

a) Are there others, family or friends, who share your use of humour?

b) What things do you laugh about together?

c) Were you/are you teased? What about? Were you laughed at?

d) What difference does humour make to your relationship/s?

3. The role of humour in diminishing, difficult situations

a) Are you able to laugh in 'serious' situations? How?

b) Are there times when laughing helps?

c) How does laughing impact on that situation?

d) What happens with this feeling that you should not laugh at certain times?

So it takes courage to laugh, because part of you says you must not.

(This is not about putting pressure on you to laugh when you want to cry.)

4. Exploring the future

a) Talking about how humour makes you feel, how long do you predict these feelings last?

b) How will you keep laughing to the forefront in difficult times? (So there is laughter as well as tears.)

c) When things are getting on top of you, what ways can you recharge your humour batteries?

d) Have you established a humour habit and made a Laughter Action Plan?

5. Making you the expert/giver

a) What advice would you give to someone else about managing stress?

b) What can you say to others about the role of humour in serious circumstances?

c) How do you help them practically when you get together?

APPENDIX 5

HOW HEALTHY IS LAUGHTER?

Laughter works on 3 levels:

1. Physical = Physiology – Your Hips!
2. Social – Your Heart!
3. Psychological = Mind – Your Head!

1. Physical – ALL BODY SYSTEMS are stimulated and strengthened: Respiratory – Circulatory – Digestive – Nervous – Musculatory – Endocrine etc. And the IMMUNE SYSTEM!
2. Social – Be a LAUGHTER CLOUD:– Drench arid zones! Laughter: Connects people, stimulates Creativity Lowers barriers and blood pressure, Opens communication, Ups oxygen levels and energy, Dissolves tension and stress.
3. Psychological – REDUCES STRESS: production of stress hormones ceases – 'pre' brain does only one thing at a time! Some stress is normal and necessary, but not chronic stress – what's that? Anticipate and manage anxiety!

It's FREE, it's EASY! No equipment or skills!

Share the Spirit of Laughter.

PURE LAUGHTER is cleansing, nourishing & healing

LAUGHTER is the most efficient, effective, and economical way to Get Healthy and stay Healthy! (It has proven long-lasting benefits)

Laughter that is based on caring & empathy helps develop resilience, and helps people cope with difficult situations.

By developing strategies to bring More FUN into your life, you:

- Fast track communication
- Unite your inner-energies!
- Nurture your relationships

Smile

Laugh often!

Lighten up – be PLAYful.

Laugh at yourself and at life!

Seek out opportunities to laugh.

You don't have to be funny, just have fun!

Develop a humorous perspective –> Perspective ->creative solutions!

By looking for the funny side –> Use Humour as a TOOL, not a weapon!

Take your WORK seriously, Not YOURSELF –> Get a Humour Habit!

APPENDIX 6

Edible Fairy Tales in 7 Rainbow Colours

Fun ways for the family to enjoy more fruit and veg!

1. RED: Little Red Apple – Good!/Little Red Raspberry/ Little Red Tomato/Sleeping Beetroot/Mary, Mary Quite Strawberry/
   Wee Willy Cherry/Rumpel-capsicum/

2. ORANGE: Cinderorange/Rumpelpumpkin/Sweet Potato/ Little Miss Melon – Muffet/There was a crooked Mango

3. YELLOW: Sleeping Banana/Goldilocks and the Three Pears/ Hansel & Grapefruit/Hansel & Lentil/Rock a Banana (Rock a Bye Baby)/Hickory Dicory Squash/Little Jack Corn Cob/Mary Had a Pineapple

4. GREEN: Beauty and the Peas/Jack and the Beans Talk-back! Hansel and Gooseberry/Hansel & Celery/Hansel & Lentil/ Three Blind Limes/Polly Put the Kiwi On/Mary Had a Cucumber/The Wheels on the Brussel Sprouts Go Round,/ The Cat and the Spinach – Hey diddle diddle/Simple Spinach (Simon)/The Prince of Broccoli –(Frogs)

5. BLUE: Baa, baa, Blueberry/Little Boy Blueberry/ Cucumber's Blue

6. PURPLE: The Three Little Figs/Hansel and Grape Bunch/ Tom, Tom the Passionfruit

7. VIOLET: Cindereggplant/Tom Plum/The Ugly Olive Also:/Rap-onion-zel/Snow White and the Seven Durians/ The Three Little Pignuts/Where, oh where is my cauliflower?/ Rub a dub-dub, rub Three coconuts/There Was an Old Mushroom That Grew in the Woods

APPENDIX 7

NOTES FOR BPL

1. NSF – The National Science Foundation, VA, USA.

2. WHO March 2017
   http://www.who.int/mediacentre/news/releases/2017/world-health-day/en/

3. Statistic from January 2012.

4. Nelson, R. (1976). Assessment and therapeutic functions of self-monitoring. In M. Hersen, R. Eisler, & P. Miller (Eds.), Progress in behavior modification, Vol. 5. New York: Academic Press. Also see Watson and Tharp (1972), Thorensen and Mahoney (1974), and Birkedahl (1990).

5. World Happiness Index http://worldhappiness.report/

6. https://www.psychologicalselfhelp.org/Chapter11.pdf

7. http://www.who.int/mediacentre/commentaries/2018/health-urban-planning/en/

8. https://lektsii.com/3-10802.html This citation is not an original source.

9. American Academy of Pediatrics:
   http://pediatrics.aappublications.org/content/129/1/e204.full?sid=1af2837a-6401-426a-a9fa-cc73b9321c39
   Professor Stuart Brown, USA, nationalinstituteforplay.org
   Professor Fraser Brown, playwales.org

10. https://www.ncbi.nlm.nih.gov/pmc/articles/PMC3505409/

11. Dr Madan Kataria, 'Laugh For No Reason'.

12. https://whole-brain.net/post-645/ and 5 other sources https://hypertextbook.com/facts/2001/JacquelineLing.shtml

13. https://www.commonsensemedia.org/research/the-common-sense-census-media-use-by-tweens-and-teenshttps://www.bbc.com/news/technology-32067158

14. Dr Madan Kataria, 'Laugh For No Reason'.

15. Hanson, Rick, Hardwiring Happiness: The New Brain Science of Contentment, Calm, and Confidence, Harmony, 2013.

16. Diamond, M. C., Krech, D., & Rosenzweig, M. R. (1964). The effects of an enriched environment on the histology of the rat cerebral cortex. Journal of Comparative Neurology.

17. https://www.health.harvard.edu/newsletter_article/why-stress-causes-people-to-overeat

18. https://neuronresearch.net/heart/&https://www.heartmath.org/research/science-of-the-heart/

19. Play Personalities created by Dr. Stuart Brown.

20. Berk, L. (1989) Neuroendocrine and stress hormone changes during mirthful laughter. American Journal of Medical Sciences, 298(6), 390–396. Fry, W. (1977). The respiratory components of mirthful laughter. Journal of Biological Psychology, 19(2), 39–50.

21. Lefcourt, H. (1986). Humor and life stress. New York: Springer-Verlag.

22. See 19 above.

23. See 21 above.

24. Fry, W. (1979). Mirth and the human cardiovascular system. In H. Mindess& J. Turek (Eds.), The study of humor (pp. 56–61). Antioch University Press.Fry, W., & Salameh, W. (Eds.). (1987). Handbook of humor and psychotherapy: Advances in the clinical use of humor. Sarasota, FL: Professional Resources. Exchange, Inc.

25. See 21 above.

26. See 21 above & Pelletier, K., & Herzing, D. (1989) Psycho-neuroimmunology: Toward a mind-body model. Advances, 5(1), 27–56.

27. https://www.painfreelivinglife.com/tools-chronic-pain/alternative-therapies/laughter-is-it-really-the-best-medicine/

28. http://www.humormatters.com/articles/heart.html
https://www.naturalnews.com/026311_laughter_humor_health.html

29. http://www.abc.net.au/science/articles/2014/12/17/4149911.htm

30. See 16 above.

31. Demos, Virginia (1995), Exploring affect: the selected writings of Silvan S. Tomkins, p. 170.

ABOUT THE AUTHOR

David Cronin is a playwright, author and Wellness 'Heartist'.

He delivers programs in Workplace Wellness and Personal Wellbeing.

David enjoys writing songs and stories and has produced twelve educational musical shows for children, as well as the controversial play, 'The Man Who Wrote Shakespeare.'

His background is in physical theatre & teaching theatre workshops. He has lived in various European and Asian countries before basing himself in Adelaide, South Australia.

He was a Clown Doctor in Adelaide for over sixteen years, where humour therapy is an integral part of the healing process.

He is Trainer & State Coordinator of Laughter Yoga Clubs SA. For over twenty years he is the principal Clown Trainer for the Adelaide Christmas Pageant.

He is a member of international bodies including the Association for Applied Therapeutic Humour, the Australian Society of Authors, the Australian Writers Guild, and the Association for Applied Improvisation.

www.davidcronin.love